EDWIN LUTYENS

APOTHEOSIS

RIBA DRAWINGS MONOGRAPHS No 1

Sketches by

EDWIN LUTYENS

MARGARET RICHARDSON

ACADEMY EDITIONS

ACKNOWLEDGEMENTS

Published in collaboration with the Royal Institute of British Architects.
All illustrative material is from the British Architectural Library, Drawings Collection, Royal Institute of British Architects.

FRONT COVER: Design for a house on the Hudson River, New York, for Mr EH Harriman, 1903, detail;
BACK COVER: Preliminary study for the Roman Catholic Metropolitan Cathedral of Christ the King,
Liverpool, c1929, detail; PAGE 2: Cartoon of Lutyens's Apotheosis showing Lutyens and his staff in 1938
when he was elected PRA, drawn by R Walker, 1938. From the left (on pediment): SW Axford, Eleanor
Webb, Percy Tribe, R Malya; (standing): R Walker, Robert Lutyens, FJ Pook, Hubert Wright, Herbert G
Bailey, Lutyens, Eric Janes, George Stewart, SG Bailey, Harold Greenwood, AR Thompson.

SERIES EDITOR: Jill Lever; MANAGING EDITOR: Maggie Toy; ART EDITOR: Andrea Bettella; CHIEF DESIGNER: Mario Bettella;
EDITORIAL TEAM: Rachel Bean, Lucy Coventry; DESIGNER: Petra Roth.
CONSULTANT: Stuart Durant

Published in Great Britain in 1994 by
ACADEMY EDITIONS an imprint of Academy Group Ltd,
42 Leinster Gardens, London W2 3AN
member of VCH PUBLISHING GROUP

Distributed to the trade in the USA by
ST MARTIN'S PRESS 175 Fifth Avenue, New York, NY 10010

ISBN: 1 85490 377 2

Printed and bound in the UK

CONTENTS

Foreword   6

Preface   7

Sketches by Lutyens   8

Plates   22

Chronology   103

Pupils, assistants and staff in the Lutyens office   104

Select Bibliography   105

List of Plates   106

Index   107

FOREWORD

Of the 80,000 or so drawings given by Sir Edwin Lutyens's son Robert to the RIBA in 1951, only 2,181 were kept. Many of these were in whole or part from the hand of Lutyens though some office, or working, drawings were kept for important schemes; in particular for the Viceroy's House, New Delhi. The loss of most of the drawings archive of England's greatest classical architect since Soane (whose own drawings have fared rather better) is tragic, and what now remains are among the most treasured drawings in the RIBA's Collection. Their presence – or absence – highlights the problem of architectural drawings in museums and record offices where their number, size and fragility can make them un-endearing.

When the 'value' of architects' drawings is discussed, it is clear that there is more than one kind of value. To Robert Lutyens, his father's drawings 'have no value in the same sense that an artist's original drawings have'. Was he thinking of monetary value or aesthetic value, or their value as records or value in the sense of allowing an insight into a highly creative mind? ASG Butler, who had sorted and saved most of what the RIBA has today, had no doubts as to their 'great artistic value', and wrote that 'they are both . . . interesting and . . .

valuable (or they will be one day)'. He appreciated all aspects of Lutyens's own drawings but not those made in the office. Scaled, ruled and compass-drawn on tracing paper and linen, they can seem impersonal, practical, technical. Yet, embodying the hundreds or thousands of design decisions that follow from the initial concept, had they survived, they would have been an incomparable record of Lutyens's built work.

In 1963, Margaret Richardson came to the RIBA Drawings Collection as Deputy Curator and, when it was suggested that she catalogue the Lutyens drawings, happily agreed to do so. Her work resulted in one of the twenty volumes of the *Catalogue of the Drawings Collection of the Royal Institute of British Architects (1969-89)* and became the basis for further publications, exhibitions and the founding of the Lutyens Trust. Now Inspectress and Assistant Curator of the Sir John Soane's Museum, I am most grateful to her for agreeing to write on Lutyens's drawings in what is to be the first of a new series of monograph books from the Drawings Collection of the Royal Institute of British Architects.

Jill Lever (Curator of the RIBA Drawings Collection)
August 1994

PREFACE

Lutyens's sketches and drawings are worn and often rather grubby – and probably always were. Mary Lutyens recalls that her father never cleaned his nails and that he would use his fingers to smudge out the soft-pencilled letters in a cross-word clue if he made a mistake. 'If he ever had a new suit,' she writes, 'it never looked new because of the ever-bulging pockets in which he kept note-pad, pencils, a knife for sharpening pencils, an India rubber, several little pipes, several boxes of matches and his tobacco pouch.' In his office Lutyens worked in a slough of loose tobacco, spent matches, bits of India rubber and unwanted instruments. Sir Hubert Worthington recalled that once 'a taxi-man arrived at the office with a dirty envelope, on which were scribbled the words "give this to Mr Worthington. It is the house for Lady So-and-so and is to be drawn out by tomorrow." He had drawn it on the way from the office to Paddington.' Over the years the sketches were rolled up and then discovered by Andrew Butler when he sorted out the Lutyens drawings for the RIBA in 1951-52. He, in turn, made his mark: he inscribed the drawings – very casually, it must be admitted – with the name of each scheme and 'Original Lutyens', 'Original EL' or 'Very early Lutyens'. Consequently, the drawings are not easy to photograph and I am most grateful to AC Cooper Ltd for taking so much trouble to produce prints which are as clear as they can make them.

I wish to acknowledge my debt to Christopher Hussey's *The Life of Sir Edwin Lutyens* (1950), Mary Lutyens's memoir of her father, *Edwin Lutyens by his Daughter* (1980) and *The Letters of Edwin Lutyens to his wife Lady Emily* (1985), edited by Clayre Percy and Jane Ridley. These letters are on loan to the RIBA Library from Jane Ridley, and I am grateful to her for allowing me to publish extracts from them and from the two sketchbooks on loan to the RIBA Drawings Collection. Mrs Angela Mace's catalogue of the letters has also been invaluable.

I want to thank Mrs Christopher Hussey for permission to quote from letters in the Hussey papers; Henry Baker to quote from a Lutyens letter in the Baker papers at the RIBA; Hilary Grainger for information about Sir Ernest George; George McHardy; Michael Barker; Eugene Rae of the Royal College of Art; Jean Duffield; and Andrew Norris and Sian Williams of the RIBA Drawings Collection.

Finally, I want to thank Jill Lever, Curator of the RIBA Drawings Collection, for asking me to write this book, which she has edited, and for her continual support, and Mary Lutyens, who generously gave the copyright for her father's drawings to the RIBA in 1980 and who has done more than anyone to help those of us who continue to be fascinated by her father's work.

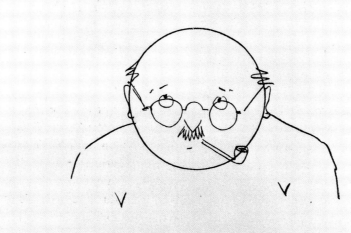

29, Bloomsbury Square.

17, Queen Anne's Gate.

7, Apple Tree Yard.

17, Bolton Street.

5, Eaton Gate.

24–2–1939.

Café Royal,
London, W.1

Menu of a dinner given at the Café Royal in honour of Lutyens becoming PRA by his former
assistants and pupils, with caricature portrait of Lutyens on cover, dated 24/2/1939.

SKETCHES BY LUTYENS

'Lutyens said to me, when I tried to describe something on the job, "Don't talk about it, draw it."'

AG Shoosmith[1]

The original sketches and drawings of Edwin Lutyens are the subject of this short study, together with an account of his office practice which enabled so many remarkable buildings to be realised. The drawings chosen are all in his own hand. They are the 'sketches', as he called them, often coloured in wash or in crayon for a client, and the ruled designs made at his drawing board.

These drawings were unknown to Andrew Butler and Christopher Hussey when they jointly prepared the text and illustrations for the *Lutyens Memorial* volumes in the late 1940s. They were tucked into the rolls of 80,000 drawings from the Lutyens office in Mansfield Street given to the RIBA by Robert Lutyens in 1951. It was Butler who volunteered to sort through the rolls in December 1951, and, in doing so, not only discovered the Lutyens schemes which were never built – the lost 'buildings on paper' – but also found several hundred original Lutyens sketches and designs, which showed him, as Butler said, to be 'an almost unrivalled artist in rough, sketch designs and sketch perspectives . . . heaps are just like things in the Uffizi!'[2] Butler worried that he and Hussey should have known about their existence before they began work on their respective volumes, as neither had ever seen the majority of the unexecuted schemes. In *The Architecture of Sir Edwin Lutyens*, Butler had focused objectively on built work, with the exception of Liverpool Cathedral, but felt that Hussey's interpretation of Lutyens's architecture in his biography, *The Life*, might have been a little different if he had known of the brilliant sketches for so many imaginative and complex architectural ideas.

In addition, there were three other important collections of drawings which were unknown to Butler and Hussey in the late 1940s. The builder, RA Wood of JW Falkner Ltd, rescued four early Lutyens sketchbooks from a dustbin in 1939 when the Lutyens office moved from No 5 Eaton Gate to No 13 Mansfield Street. Then Robert Lutyens gave a small group of his father's earliest designs, including those made at the South Kensington School of Art to his partner, Harold Greenwood, in 1953. Greenwood had been devoted to Lutyens and had done much to keep the office going in the 1930s; after his death Mrs Greenwood sold them to the RIBA, together with one hundred and thirty-four early sketches for Liverpool Cathedral, which Greenwood had preserved. Finally, a group of early sketches for different schemes and a virtually complete set of working drawings for Liverpool Cathedral were found to be in George Stewart's collection, which was acquired by the RIBA in 1980. He had been with Lutyens from 1911 to the end and had later drawn the illustrations for the *Memorial* volumes.

It is the purpose of this book, therefore, to publish a selection of these original sketches to complement the work of Butler and Hussey in their *Memorial* volumes of nearly fifty years ago.

Lutyens, like Robert Adam and Le Corbusier, had a gift for drawing and painting that went beyond architecture. But, unlike Adam and Le Corbusier, who channelled their creative energies into Picturesque landscapes or Cubist paintings, Lutyens rarely sketched buildings or landscapes in a topographical sense or produced paintings as works of art. He drew constantly, however, illustrating letters in a spontaneous and pictorial way with doodles and figures, plans and ideas. He also produced 'vivreations', Lutyens's word for all light-hearted activities, in the form of drawings to amuse his children, friends and clients. This gift meant that he was able, from an early age, to realise his concepts on paper and to see 'in the round'. For Lutyens would rarely talk about architecture although his visual memory was phenomenal; he knew St Paul's by heart and absorbed what he wanted from buildings in the past without feeling the need to sketch them. He could also draw from dictation. Hussey describes the episode when he drew up the designs which were dictated by an old, blind Sapper and how he later recommended this exercise to the Cambridge Architectural Society in 1932.[3]

In spite of this, Lutyens doubted his own draughtsmanship, particularly in his early years, just as he regretted his lack of a public school education. When his wife, Lady Emily, reported in 1900 that Lord Battersea, Lutyens's client for The Pleasaunce at Overstrand, had said that he was 'the finest draughtsman he had ever seen', Lutyens replied, 'What rot Lord B saying that about my draughtsmanship. I *don't* like it!! It is so insincere and untrue.'[4] Lutyens also wrote to Herbert Baker in 1903 saying that he had made sketches for a job he wanted in three days but that he feared they were 'no match in draughtsmanship'.[5] Consequently, with an amused contempt for professionalism, Lutyens presented himself as a self-taught architect – an image which did not entirely match up with his background and early training.

For Lutyens had inherited art. He was born on 29 March 1869, at No 16 Onslow Square, London, one of thirteen children, the son of Mary Gallwey and Charles Henry Augustus Lutyens. Charles Lutyens began his career in the army and was sent to Canada in 1848 where he met his wife. Like many artillerymen and engineers, he had been trained in draughtsmanship and showed unusual talent; he made watercolour drawings of Niagara Falls and other places in Canada, and of the country around Sebastopol when his regiment was later ordered to the Crimea in 1855. He was also inventive and in 1857 made a reflecting instrument for judging distances for long-range artillery, called a stadiometer which was used throughout the service for nearly forty years. This inventiveness was matched by an early design made by Edwin, or Ned as he was called as a child, inscribed 'Design/ by/ Edwin Landseer Lutyens' for a 'Twin-Screw Engine for Torpedo Boats & Launches'.[6]

In 1857 Charles Lutyens retired from the army and took up painting professionally in London. He went to study with Sir Edwin Landseer, who by January 1859 was sharing a studio in Onslow Square with the sculptor Baron Carlo Marochetti and working on the four bronze lions that surround the base of Nelson's Column in Trafalgar Square. Charles is said to have helped with these lions; Landseer certainly became a good friend and godfather of Ned Lutyens. Charles himself became a successful painter of animal subjects, landscapes, portraits and hunting scenes and exhibited from 1862 to 1903 at the Royal Academy and was hung 'on the line'. He was particularly successful in the 1870s and '80s with commissions through Landseer to paint the portraits and horses of many rich clients including the Prince of Wales and the Duke of Westminster. Two striking paintings of horses and carriages set against the architectural background of the Royal Mews belong to the Grosvenor Estate and are dated 1884. This success enabled Charles to buy a substantial house – somewhat inappropriately called The Cottage – at Thursley in Surrey in 1876, which gave him access to a wider range of clients through his hunting connections. He already knew some of the aesthetic set in London as the architect EW Godwin is noted as being a visitor to Onslow Square in 1879,[7] and in Surrey he also met Randolph Caldecott, who moved to Frensham near Farnham in 1882. By the 1890s, however, Charles Lutyens's earnings had dwindled and the family became very poor. He began to go blind and to practise strange economies, as Mary Lutyens relates in her memoir of her father, *Edwin Lutyens by His Daughter*. Perhaps, as she suggests, it was these signs of poverty and disorder at home that disturbed Lutyens so profoundly that he rarely referred to his father or to his paintings. All his life he was terrified of ending up in the same circumstances.

Ned Lutyens spent half his time as a child in Thursley and half in London. As a result of rheumatic fever he was considered too delicate to go away to public school – although he did go to a day school in London for two years. Instead he spent a good deal of time in the country looking at old buildings and spending time in the village carpenter's shop and at Tickner's, the local builder's yard at Godalming, or on jobs where they were working. He is said to have invented a transparent sketchbook, which was a sheet of glass. This he held up to the building, sketching its outline with a sharpened piece of soap.

Lutyens later used to say that Randolph Caldecott's drawings first turned his eyes to architecture. He said that Caldecott 'found a new simplicity of expression in the buildings he so wittily portrayed'.[8] Caldecott was the illustrator of sixteen picture books printed in colour by Edmund Evans in the 1870s and '80s. In these and in his even more striking illustrations for the *Daily Graphic* Caldecott achieved a new kind of unaffected spontaneity which obviously appealed to Lutyens and which he later emulated. The backgrounds in his drawings have Georgian or half-timbered cottages; the interiors are furnished with settles and dressers, with Windsor and Georgian chairs. In a similar way to Kate Greenaway, Caldecott looked back to the simple, country Georgian period, a world with old-fashioned flowers and 'the good work of old days' that Lutyens came to admire.

In 1885, before his sixteenth birthday in March, Lutyens was sent as a fee-paying student to the South Kensington School of Art – or to the National Art Training School as it had been known since 1864. It is likely that he did so on the advice of Caldecott, whose closest friend, the decorative painter Thomas Armstrong, had become Director of Art at South Kensington in 1881. Lutyens did not go to the school purely to study architecture, as has often been stated, although his training did include a certain number of architectural subjects. He would have had to work his way through a series of stages or exercises, drawn up by Richard Redgrave in 1852, which were designed to equip the art teacher or amateur with sufficient technique to teach or to pursue a technical craft. These stages consisted of geometrical drawing with the aid of instruments, drawing from flat examples or casts, shading from round or solid forms, painting ornament and modelling before reaching the last stage which was composition in design in itself.

Although Lutyens left before finishing the course he would have acquired a good foundation in the syntax of drawing, sculpture and ornament. Besides Walter Crane, the designer, Edward Lantéri, one of the proponents of the 'new sculpture', also taught at the school, which may account for Lutyens's later technical knowledge of the uses and value of sculpture and applied craft in his work. Harold Falkner, the Arts and Crafts architect, for example, wrote to Hussey in 1953,

> A thing not emphasised in the *Life* is EL's extraordinary influence on his craftsmen – viz Broadbent's carving at Maytham and Marshcourt and the CL offices. I saw the drawings of Gt M – the carving is merely suggested yet no one else got such carving out of Abraham Broadbent. Also Müntzer's furnishing at Temple Dinsley, I doubt if he did anything like as well for anyone else.[9]

His early training at South Kensington might also have accounted for his reaction to Lady Emily's suggestion in 1912 that their son, Robert, should have painting lessons.

> I will ask Tonks about Robert. He is Head of the Slade School. What I should like Robert to learn would be geometry and sciography [*sic*], the science of drawing shadows. To know what shapes a shadow would be. The shadow a steeple throws on a dome! You see the oddity of it all in one's own shadow where it falls on rough ground and half against an upright wall – or a bank etc. But it is no use to start off painting pictures. I don't mean to discourage it – but it is not serious unless it teaches observation and to know the discovered facts helps observation enormously . . .[10]

An early set of drawings at the RIBA, acquired from Mrs Greenwood in 1973, show some of Lutyens's architectural exercises at South Kensington. There are designs for a 'Queen Anne' boat house (plate 1), a 'Classical Baroque' public library, an 'Old English' tennis club and a 'Second Empire' town hall – probably all made as part of a course in architectural styles. There are also four boards of topographical sketches of buildings made in Normandy in the August of either 1885, 1886 or 1887 – while he was at South Kensington as they are mounted on boards as presentation sets of architectural sketches. Board 1 has a torn label inscribed '1st prize'. These and other drawings in the Greenwood collection, as well as remarks in an early letter to his mother where he says: 'I hope to be down at Easter and hope to go on with sketching excursions harder than ever, and I hope to benefit by the experience obtained last summer',[11] show that in his early years Lutyens did go sketching in spite of his later scorn for sketchbooks.

By this date, about 1885-86, Lutyens was already determined to become a 'successful architect'. In September 1886, the Earl of Home, who was probably a client of his father, generously offered the design problem of enlarging The Hirsel in Berwickshire. Lutyens responded with characteristic confidence, 'it is one of the most interesting I have ever had', suggesting a scheme of enormous scale to transform the fenestration of the existing house. Not surprisingly it was never carried out but it was his first realistic design project.[12]

In the following year, in late 1887, Lutyens entered the office of Sir Ernest George and Peto as an articled pupil, where he formed important friendships with Herbert Baker, Guy Dawber and R Weir Schultz, who were all assistants there at the time. At that date George's office was one of the busiest architectural practices in England, best known for the 'Dutch' houses in Harrington and Collingham Gardens in Kensington, and for large country houses such as Batsford Park, Gloucestershire. In 1887 the office was at No 18 Maddox Street, on the first floor, in rooms panelled in oak in a Dutch style, the walls covered with gold-framed drawings in watercolour and sepia wash. There were no curtains but shutters, decorated with elaborate hinges and spring centres of early Flemish design. George undertook all the designing himself, while Harold Peto dealt with all other aspects of professional life. The pupils and assistants, ranging in number from six to twelve, drew up George's sketches to scale, and traced and produced the working drawings. A man called Gould acted as the office manager, kept the accounts and dealt with the quantity surveyors and subcontractors.

George was always interested in quality and his buildings were expensive, often very expensive. His pupils were taught to value high quality in materials and craftsmanship although such ideas were not presented as tenets of an Arts and Crafts philosophy. In his RIBA Presidential address to students in 1909, George said that 'the arts of building and architecture cannot be separated', and argued that, ideally, an architect should be 'a good joiner, mason and worker in metal' but, realistically, could not spare the time 'to grow efficient in various crafts'. Nevertheless, he maintained 'when drawing a moulding the architect should have stone, oak or plaster in his mind'. He encouraged students to 'use every opportunity of visiting works in progress, builders' workshops and masons' yards'.[13]

Lutyens inherited much of this philosophy, as did Baker and Dawber, although he later rather scorned George's love of sketching, recalling:

a distinguished architect who took each year a three week's holiday abroad and returned with overflowing sketchbooks. When called on for a project he would look through these and choose some picturesque turret or gable from Holland, France or Spain, and round it weave his new design. Location mattered little, and no provincial formation influenced him, for at that time terracotta was the last word in building. All honour to Philip Webb and Norman Shaw for their gallant attempt to bring England back to craftsmanship and tradition.[14]

In 1888 Lutyens had a reputation for building wattle and daub cowsheds and other constructions, so he would not have appreciated George's reliance on foreign prototypes. In other respects, however, he learnt a good deal from George. His office was later to be organised on similar lines. He learnt how to make working drawings and full-sizes for quality carvers and metalworkers, some of whom, like J Starkie Gardner, also worked for Lutyens. George also taught Lutyens to design and draw in a pictorial manner, for soft, sepia perspectives, often drawn from a low viewpoint, were his speciality.

In early 1889 Lutyens received his first commission of any consequence, Crooksbury House near Farnham in Surrey for the Chapmans. This enabled him to leave George and to set up on his own – even though his 'office' was only his bedroom at No 16 Onslow Square, which, as he said 'he had fitted up with Dutch shutters and an oversized and overhanging fireplace.'[15] His drawings of this period show the easy informality in setting out a design (plate 4) as well as the professionalism he must have acquired in the George office (plate 6). His first exhibited work at the Royal Academy (from an address, No 28 Craven Street, rather than his father's address at Onslow Square), was his preliminary design for Crooksbury, which he chose to illustrate with a line drawing by Leonard Martin rather than his own watercolour perspective (plate 5).

In late 1893 Lutyens was able to take two, white-panelled rooms for an office at No 6 Gray's Inn Square, very much an architects' enclave. His first assistant was the aged and pious William 'Billie' Barlow, who had been a builder and clerk of works, and who was recommended to Lutyens by John Sparkes, Principal of South Kensington School of Art. We know comparatively little of the years 1889-96 as Lutyens's correspondence with his future wife, Lady Emily Lytton, only began in September 1896. We do know that he coped virtually single-handed with an important range of early jobs. Some of these, from the years 1892 to 1894, he recorded in a series of thumb-nail sketches made to send to Herbert Baker in South Africa; his record sketch of Chinthurst Hill (plate 13) is a good example. He later recalled the intensity of this period,

> I went to no parties, I knew no one and worked till 12-2 in the morning. I bicycled a lot and walked a good bit, but no sport and no relaxation; just work.[16]

Lutyens often presented his designs at this time in small sketchbooks, as if the drawings in them represented views of built work rather than designs for projected buildings. Six of these sketchbooks survive. Two of them, containing pencil surveys, belong to the Wood family of the late JW Falkner Ltd; the third, the Fulbrook sketchbook,[17] belongs to the Lutyens Trust. The Munstead Corner sketchbook, datable to 1891, is now at the Victoria and Albert Museum, and the Munstead Wood and Castle-in-the-Air sketchbooks are on loan to the RIBA. The watercolours in four of them were made for clients and are closer in character to the watercolours of artists like Helen Allingham and Birket Foster than to contemporary architectural drawings of this period. In two of the books (for Munstead Corner and Munstead Wood) Lutyens was able to project his imagination into the life to be led in the houses in a way that was similar to the drawings of Caldecott (plate 10).

By early 1897 Lutyens had Barlow and three pupils, HL North, Robert Marchant and WH Ward; Maxwell Ayrton is mentioned in June and by late September he had seven in all. On 25 September he planned to take on a secretary – Dalton, 'a first class character from Col Spencer', who went 'all thro' the Berber campaign with the Camel Corps – a soldier – and no vices'.[18] From the start Lutyens had difficulty in controlling his men. As he wrote to Lady Emily on 5 February 1897,

> I have given my men a warm half hour here. They ask such stupid questions. I was *not* cross! only very dictatorial and impressive using Bump-sicaical language. They never realise that a working drawing is merely a letter to a builder telling him precisely what is required of him and not a picture wherewith to charm an idiotic client.[19]

A good example of a 'letter to a builder' was his design for Shere lodge (plate 12), which with its plans, elevations and two perspectives from different angles, gives a three-dimensional view of the building in a straightforward manner. Because he believed that drawings were working documents, Lutyens did not like any kind of embellishment at the working drawing stage. 'Don't portmanteau it' was the standard criticism of an overcrowded sheet. Much later, in the 1930s, Hal Kent remembers that he drew a border around his first drawing there. Lutyens drew in a little figure looking round it and said, 'What does the builder do with this?'[20] Lutyens knew only too well that the choice of a contractor who knew how to build with first-class materials, coupled with a clerk of works on site and close supervision by the architect, was far more important than academic draughtsmanship.

On 4 August 1897 Lutyens married Lady Emily Lytton. Before he had been able to do so, he had demonstrated to the Lytton family that his income was steadily increasing and agreed to take out a life insurance for £11,000. The pressure on him to find work was considerable, especially as he had set his heart on leasing No 29 Bloomsbury Square as his new home and office:

> The house is beautiful – large, airy rooms, beautiful mantelpieces and staircase. You enter a square hall and a beautiful staircase is beyond; three rooms which the great Norman Shaw used as his offices! during his busiest period! Such lovely doorways and cornices everywhere.

He also noted his expenses in the same letter:

> House £200, taxes £60, Assurance £190, Living £500, Clerks £400, odds and ends £100; Total £1450. This means £29,000 worth of work in a year which I ought to get.[21]

Lutyens had already, in his constant scramble for work, increased the number of jobs undertaken in the office: in 1897 alone he worked on twenty-five different schemes, including five new houses – Fulbrook, Berrydown, Orchards, Sullingstead and The Pleasaunce, Overstrand; in 1898 he worked on ten, including Goddards and Le Bois des Moutiers. A letter of 27 May 1897 to Lady Emily gives some idea of his subconscious hopes at this time. Gertrude Jekyll had written to say that she wanted to see him about something 'rather mysterious'. 'Oh love, what can it mean?', wrote Lutyens,

> Someone wants to give me an enormous job! Some rich body wants to adopt us and give us £40,000 a year. The Duke of Westminster wants to give me some appointment? G Balfour?? Princess Louise wants to know if I would rebuild Windsor and should she give my name to her Mamma? What can it be, love?[22]

The answer was the commission to build Orchards.

The office moved to No 29 Bloomsbury Square in October 1897, where it occupied the whole ground floor of the house. The front room was Lutyens's private office and communicating with it was the main drawing office where the assistants worked. At the back was a small room, first occupied by Badcock and later by AJ Thomas. For, by 1898 Lutyens badly needed a business manager to handle the technical and financial side of his practice. So he took E Baynes Badcock into a kind of partnership on the understanding that he could take work on his own account, using identical writing paper with his own name instead of Lutyens's on it, whilst acting as his technical partner at the same time. Badcock was a persuasive talker and a Cambridge blue, as well as owning a share in a firm of builders, Badcock and Maxey, who had built Fulbrook. By early 1901 things were not going well between them. Lutyens felt that Badcock neglected his work and made a mess of the jobs he was involved with. Badcock, in turn, wanted to be introduced to clients, which Lutyens was reluctant to do as Badcock then behaved in a familiar way and 'like a cad'. Consequently Badcock terminated his agreement and left by the end of March. On 12 April Lutyens wrote that a large tombstone had been made for Badcock in the office, 'In memory of EBB, for three years sleeping partner at BS, died of talking and from doing no work'. Lutyens was deeply upset by this, but what hurt him even more was to hear that by July in the same year Badcock was building for his carefully nurtured client, Princess Louise.

This was not an easy period, for Dalton, his secretary, 'the first class character from Col Spencer', bolted with the office cash and a housemaid. Order was restored, however, in the following year, 1902, when AJ Thomas became his new office manager. Thomas continued to work as his trusted right-hand man for thirty-three years and together with Edward Hall (who also came in 1902 and stayed until 1933) and George Stewart (who came in 1911 and remained until the end), became the main props of the office. Without them Lutyens could never have achieved such a large number of finely detailed buildings. Right from the start Thomas was allowed to do work on his own account, in lieu of part of his salary. This was a similar arrangement to Badcock's and led to misunderstandings in the 1930s. Thomas was never popular with the men, but this was probably understandable as he was keeper of the purse and discipline rested with him.

Nonetheless, Lutyens trusted him with the office and left everything in his hands when he went to Delhi, giving him power of attorney.

After 1902 the method of work in the office developed into an accustomed routine. Lutyens always stood at his drawing board in the front room, very erect and slim (as shown in the Phipps sketch (page 21)), and usually smoking a pipe. Oswald Milne remembered that 'Lutyens never explained himself; his wonderful fund of ideas and invention were expressed not in speech but at the end of a pencil.'[23] Once he had settled on a design he would pass it to a pupil to draw to scale. If the men were in difficulties they would invite him to come and help them out. He would then put a piece of tracing paper over the drawing, and in a minute or two, had sketched half a dozen solutions to the problem. He then put a ring around the one he preferred and left them to carry it out. Lutyens was extremely shy with his pupils and once said, 'They terrify me!'[24] He often corrected their drawings late at night; at other times he could be severely critical.

Hussey explained that they learnt from what they saw by watching Lutyens drawing and experimenting:

Since his spontaneous conceptions were in small and ostensibly rough drawings, which the assistant had to scale and draw up with all the niceties that contribute so much to the individuality of a Lutyens building, each of these young men came to be convinced that he himself shared direct responsibility in evolving them. He felt that he was helping to create architectural forms that would be studied and measured by future generations.[25]

As Lutyens turned increasingly, as he did in the early 1900s, to what he called the 'high game', an inventive game that was based on the classical language of architecture, it meant, as he admitted, 'hard labour, hard thinking, over every line in all three dimensions and in every joint; and no stone can be allowed to slide'.[26] This 'hard thinking' is reflected in many of his drawings of this period (for example in plates 26 and 32), and increasingly from this time onwards he wrestled with his ideas on a pad of graph paper, often using crayon to heighten the effect. He also drew constantly on pads which were specially made for him, called 'virgins', which fitted into his pockets. Often clients would watch fascinated as their house appeared to grow and develop on paper. This could, however, be an illusion; Lutyens worked so rapidly that the house had probably already taken shape in his mind and already been explored at his drawing board.

Oswald Milne recalled the occasion when Lutyens got back to London after visiting Little Thakeham. He handed Milne:

> two sheets of squared paper with the house completely worked out in sketch form with all the plans, sections and elevations. He must have done the whole thing in the train. He asked me to get to work at once on the scale drawings. Little Thakeham as built is almost exactly to the sketch which he made in that way.'[27]

Surviving at the RIBA, however, are several sheets of sketches for the house (plate 29) which show that Lutyens did not reach the final design so easily. Similarly, Lady Sackville believed that she had five sketch designs for the Cenotaph which Lutyens had made for her at dinner in July 1919. It is more likely that the sketches were re-workings of earlier ideas.[28]

When his assistants had to draw up his sketches to scale, they did so by applying a system of ratios and proportions which Lutyens had evolved and which gave the distinctive character to all his work. Hussey explains that:

> these ratios were not conceived in the abstract. In the first instance they were evolved by trial and error to justify visual preference and were converted into mathematical formula secondly. They were arrived at mainly by juggling with his sketch design, in which he conceived the rough proportion required. If the stock ratio, as given in the text book or by previous usage, did not meet the case, the design was delicately adjusted until the required mathematically inevitable ratio emerged.[29]

Or often an assistant was told to go and work up a design with the aid of the office 'bible' – Batty Langley, three office copies of which survive.

On 20 August 1910 the office moved to No 17 Queen Anne's Gate, where it occupied three floors of barren and grubby rooms, Lutyens's being on the first floor at the back adjoining the main drawing office at the front. Although Lutyens now had a new team of fee-paying pupils and assistants, AJ Thomas and Edward Hall remained to administer the office as Lutyens increasingly spent more time abroad. On 28 March 1912 he left on the first of nineteen journeys to Delhi, often spending between three and five months away each year. In the spring of 1913 he opened a separate Delhi office in London at No 7 Apple Tree Yard, in the upper part of the mews behind No 7 St James's Square, which the Farrers let him have as they did not at the time require accommodation for a chauffeur. Edward Hall became its manager, and assistants remember the regular panics to meet the deadlines to get large rolls of working drawings to the India Office by 4 o'clock in time to catch the boat train.

Then came the War. Twelve men in his office volunteered for service and even Mr Tribe, Lutyens's 'groom-porter' offered himself as a constable. Queen Anne's Gate was sublet, with the work doubling up with that of Delhi at Apple Tree Yard, until 1919 when it reopened. Lutyens had less work and a smaller staff than he had had since his marriage in 1897. There were only William Wands and Clare Nauheim as draughtsmen in 1918, with Thomas as manager and Hall dealing with Delhi – such as it was. From April 1917 no fresh building work was put in hand there until the end of the War, which represented a considerable financial loss to Lutyens.

In spite of the great creative and personal success of the Cenotaph, Lutyens had an overdraft of £6,000 in 1920 and remained constantly anxious about money throughout the 1920s. He was burdened by supertax and particularly by an unexpected claim in 1929 to pay thousands of pounds in back taxes. Lutyens never employed an accountant and it is thought that Edward Hall may have filled in the Delhi tax returns inaccurately. Hall was unworldly and no businessman. However, after the War work built up and was of a scale and complexity that Lutyens had not experienced before, except at Delhi. The building of Britannic House in the City in 1920 involved Thomas in a good deal of technical negotiations with the planners and London Underground; afterwards Lutyens did all his commercial work in collaboration with other architects, who took on most of the internal planning, working drawings and general supervision. Then there were the numerous private memorials, which were experiments in abstraction on a small scale (plates 78 and 79), and the complex geometrical compositions of the war cemeteries and Memorials to the Missing. Many of the working drawings for these memorials are in Lutyens's own hand and give a good idea of the geometric forms and set-backs he used (plates 65 and 70). As one of the principal architects to the Imperial War Graves Commission, he received a salary of £600 a year after 1919, although his work in an advisory capacity was given for free. Delhi, of course, continued – as did his domestic work – and in the midst of all this, in the early 1920s, he took on the task of designing and co-ordinating the Queen's Dolls' House, which was actually built at Apple Tree Yard.

In the early 1920s the Head Office was still at No 17 Queen Anne's Gate, although in 1924 the Delhi office moved to No 17 Bolton Street. Both offices then combined in 1931, moving to No 5 Eaton Gate where they remained until 1939, when one office was installed at the back of No 13 Mansfield Street. Although the same routines and the same spirit prevailed as it had at Bloomsbury Square, Lutyens himself was more revered as the 'old man'. Things were also a good deal more efficiently run with Eleanor Webb as secretary and Thomas as manager.

Lutyens spent every morning at head-office and the afternoons at the Delhi office. At both there was a steady stream of assistants bringing the results of the previous day's work for his approval or emendation. Inevitably, there are many more memories of these two last decades.

Bertram Carter, who was a pupil from 1919 to 1922 (and later went on to be Treasurer of the

MARS Group), remembered Lutyens's kindness in never correcting their actual drawings; he would instead carefully sketch in the correction on a long roll of tracing paper placed over them. This was unusual in terms of current office practice and recalled with gratitude.

My first shock upon completing my pupilship was to enter the office of Yates, Cook and Darbyshire, then in the process of destroying Regent Street. Fewer drawings were done for a whole job than Sir Edwin would devote to a dormer window . . . My first job was to trace the Cenotaph drawings, the elevations of which batter to a point 900 (or 1,000) feet up. All set-backs differed as they ascended and of course the end elevations receded more quickly than the main ones. One dimension I remember was, I think, $1' \ 7\frac{37}{40}''$ or something like that; it could not be worked in Portland stone but it had to be correct.[30]

Robert Heal, who was in the Delhi office at Bolton Street from 1927 to 1930, remembered that the work was often tedious – transferring a full set of plans up to $\frac{1}{8}$th scale, but he knew of no other architect with the same breadth of intellect as Lutyens. He was endlessly inventive: he would design something, consider the first idea too obvious and then move on to a more subtle solution in the end. Lutyens was like an eighteenth-century gentleman: the worst thing he could ever say about anyone was that he bet 'he lived with his wife in a bedsitter'.[31]

Hal Kent, a South African architect, entered Lutyens's office at Eaton Gate in mid-1935 and left at the end of 1937. The Liverpool Cathedral office was in the front room on the first floor with Lutyens's own drawing office at the rear. Kent greatly enjoyed his time there and got on well with the 'old man', largely because he could hold his own and struck the pose of the 'wild colonial', as Lutyens called him. Many of the men, though, went in awe of Lutyens. While he was there Kent worked principally on the Cathedral but also on the Villers-Bretoneux Cemetery, the Irish War Memorial in Dublin, Hore-Belisha's house at No 16 Stafford Place and Middleton Park. Lutyens was an absolute perfectionist in detailing, and drawings had to be redrawn countless times for details like diminishing brickwork at Villers-Bretoneux, and adjustment of planes at the Cathedral.

The office did not generally do perspectives, but on one occasion when Kent drew one for the Looe Hotel scheme (1936), Lutyens told him to draw his trees to look like men taking off their shirts. It was then sent round to Cyril Farey to be coloured in. Lutyens was very fussy about colour and believed it should be applied to a drawing like a good chef breathes garlic over his soup. He used William Walcot and Cyril Farey as his perspective artists. Generally Lutyens preferred Walcot – particularly admiring the 'heat' he managed to give his Delhi buildings – but later came to use Farey increasingly, as he said you could walk into a Farey building.

Lutyens took great pride in the Cathedral. Kent once asked him why he did not use reinforced concrete for the Crypt stairs and Lutyens replied that concrete had only been tested for a hundred years. When Kent left in 1937 Lutyens encouraged him to go saying, 'You don't want to work for an old man', and gave him an introduction to Corbett in New York. He gave his assistants very good references.[32]

There are, as we have seen, certain characteristics in Lutyens's drawings. The bird's-eye perspectives focused on the roofs of buildings. Lutyens often told his pupils always to design the roof first. He once flew over London in 1935 and noted with glee that his Hampton Court Bridge looked so much better than any other.[33] He was always keen to look at things from what he called 'God's point of view' and the bird's-eyes helped him to do this.

By contrast, a low viewpoint underscored the monumentality of a design. This was given a tangible reality in his built work by the use of set-backs, batter and diminishing masonry and brickwork.

Then Lutyens's drawings often show an ability to project his imagination into the life his clients might lead in a building or, perhaps, ought to lead. He could visualise and furnish an interior and often did so in his drawings – for example in the Munstead Wood sketchbook or in a series of designs he made for Captain Day.[34]

Finally, Lutyens combined plans, elevations, sections and perspectives to create a cohesive, integrated design, often drawing as a sculptor or painter might, an ability he had possibly inherited from his father. Although he rarely, if ever, referred to his father's work or to his early training at South Kensington, in 1937-38 he put some thought into defining a prospectus for a School of Architecture. He said that 'its *raison d'être* and its essential difference from any system of training at the present in use, is just this: it will attempt to turn the student, not into a specialist, but into an artist'. The emphasis of the whole course of training would be on practical rather than theoretical knowledge, but architecture must be placed among the arts, particularly painting for its 'harmony and contrast in colour, balance in design and sense of texture' and sculpture for its 'sense of form and mass and rhythm'.[35]

Lutyens's ability to draw in three dimensions enabled him to realise the great Memorials to the Missing and the even more complex design for Liverpool Cathedral. He spent the last decade of his life working on the Cathedral project and died on 1 January 1944 at Mansfield Street, surrounded by his Cathedral drawings, which he had asked Miss Webb to bring up to his room and arrange round the walls so that he could study them.

NOTES

1 AG Shoosmith, 'Reminiscences on Sir Edwin Lutyens', *Architectural Association Journal*, LXXIV, 1959, p234.

2 ASG Butler, letter to Christopher Hussey, 23 April 1952. Hussey papers, Scotney Castle.

3 Christopher Hussey, *The Life of Sir Edwin Lutyens*, 1950, pp21-22.

4 Lady Emily to Lutyens, 13 August 1900; Lutyens to Lady Emily, 15 August 1900. Lutyens letters, RIBA.

5 Lutyens to Herbert Baker, 15 February 1903. Baker papers, RIBA.

6 RIBA Lutyens Catalogue [341].

7 EW Godwin's sketchbook, dated 22 November 1878 to June 1879, (V & A, E 248 – 1963), p18, shows a sketch portrait of a young girl, inscribed 'At Lutyens/March 1879'. The girl could be one of Lutyens's two sisters and the nature of the sketch shows that Godwin could have visited the Lutyens household as a family friend. Godwin's own drawings prefigure Lutyens's in their informality and he may have influenced Lutyens's work, particularly in interior decoration. (Information from Jill Lever).

8 Sir Edwin Lutyens, Foreword, '1874 and After', *The Architectural Review*, LXX, 1931, p91.

9 Harold Falkner, letter to Christopher Hussey, 27 July 1953. Hussey papers, Scotney Castle.

10 Lutyens to Lady Emily, 5 September 1912. Lutyens letters, RIBA.

11 Lutyens to his mother, *c*1885, quoted in Christopher Hussey, *op cit*, 1950, pp12-13.

12 Quoted in *Lutyens*, Arts Council exhibition catalogue, 1981, p59.

13 Sir Ernest George, Address to students, *RIBA Journal*, XVI, 1908-9, pp225-230.

14 Christopher Hussey, *op cit*, p17.

15 Mary Lutyens, *Edwin Lutyens by his Daughter*, 1980, p20.

16 Christopher Hussey, *op cit*, 1950, p21.

17 Published in facsimile, Jane Brown (ed), *Fulbrook, The Sketchbook, Letters, Specification of Works & Accounts for a House by Edwin Lutyens, 1896-1899*, 1989.

18 Lutyens to Lady Emily, 25 September 1897. Lutyens letters, RIBA.

19 'Bumpsicaical' refers to the rather fierce language Gertrude Jekyll might have used. Lutyens called her 'Bumps'.

20 Notes made by the author of a conversation with Hal Kent, 16 October 1980.

21 Lutyens to Lady Emily, 14 July 1897. Lutyens letters, RIBA.

22 Gerald Balfour (1853-1945) married Lady Emily's sister, Lady Betty Lytton, in 1887. He was the brother of Arthur Balfour, Irish Chief Secretary and President of the Board of Trade, 1900-05. Princess Louise (1848-1939) was the fourth daughter of Queen Victoria. Lutyens met her in 1896.

23 Oswald P Milne, 'Reminiscences on Sir Edwin Lutyens', *Architectural Association Journal*, LXXIV, 1959, p232.

24 Lutyens to Lady Emily, 8 October 1906. Lutyens letters, RIBA.

25 Christopher Hussey, *op cit*, p164.

26 Christopher Hussey, *op cit*, p133

27 Oswald P Milne, *op cit*, p232.

28 The sketches are now at the Imperial War Museum.

29 Christopher Hussey, *op cit*, p164.

30 Notes by Bertram Carter of his pupilship, November 1919 to November 1922, sent to the author, 1981.

31 Notes made by the author of a conversation with Robert Heal, 1981.

32 Notes made by the author of a conversation with Hal Kent, 16 October 1980.

33 Lutyens to Lady Emily, 3 September 1935. Lutyens letters, RIBA.

34 The designs for Captain Day's house, now at the RIBA, were published in Margaret Richardson, *Lutyens and the Sea Captain*, Scolar Press (London), 1981.

35 Unpublished typescript, Laurence Whistler, 'Rough Prospectus Got Out From Sir Edwin Lutyens' Notes at his Request', *c*1937-38. Hussey papers, Scotney Castle.

Hon Paul Phipps (1880-1953)
Caricature of Lutyens and his pupils and assistants, *c*1902. From the left: Lutyens, SH Evans, Oswald P Milne, P Phipps, Wallich, AJ Thomas, 'IP' (Infant Prodigy) Huddart, G Alwyn.

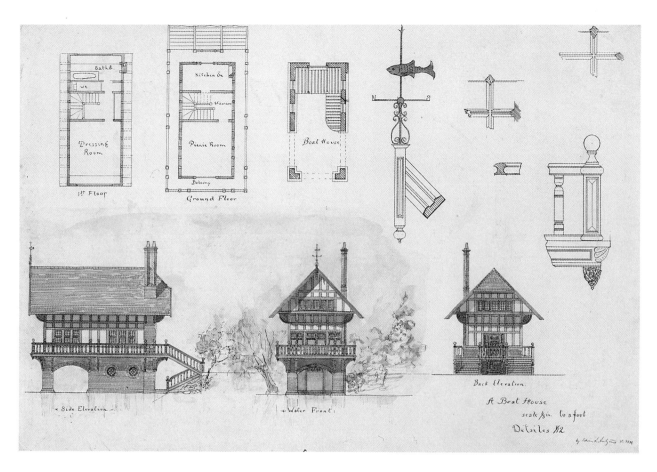

1. **Design for a boat-house, *c*1885-87**

Pen and coloured wash (420 × 630)

This scheme was one of the design projects made by Lutyens at the South Kensington School of Art, which he entered in 1885 at the age of sixteen. Its style resembles, with its use of half-timbering and verandahs, the holiday version of 'Queen Anne' found at seaside resorts, cricket pavilions, boat-houses and riverside residences all over the country in the 1870s and '80s.

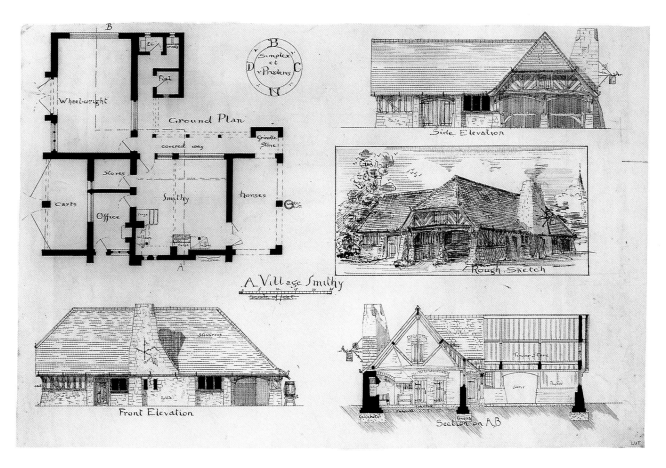

Labels within drawing:

Ground Plan
Simplex et Prudens
Wheel-wright
Fuel
Stores
Carts
Office
Smithy
horses
Grindle Stone
covered way
A Village Smithy
Scale of feet

Side Elevation

Rough Sketch

Front Elevation

Section on A B

2. Competition design for a village smithy for the *Building News* Designing Club, early 1888

Pen (355 × 565)

Submitted under the motto 'Simplex et Prudens', this drawing is the first to show Lutyens's interest in designs based on vernacular buildings. It was placed in the second class, the *Building News* commenting that the architect 'draws badly but has a notion of rural architecture and the advantage of simple lines in such buildings'. The drawing, it is true, differs from the academic presentation of the exhibition rooms but shows Lutyens's emerging, informal, personal style as well as his early ability to capture the essential forms of a functional building.

3. **Competition design for a country house, 1888**

Pen and coloured wash (440 × 775)

Lutyens won the National Bronze Medal for this design, which is one of a set of seven sheets. He was aged nineteen. As a drawing it is assured and formal in its presentation, following the hard-ruled manner of the Shaw office. Its architecture is also close to Shaw's 'Old English' and has particular echoes of Pierrepont and Merrist Wood in Surrey, which Lutyens would have known well. His use of Gothic traceried windows, however, was a personal motif which he later repeated at Chinthurst Hill (plate 13) and Castle Drogo (plate 47). The Tudor bay at the south-west end also anticipates what was to come later at the Buckhurst Park music room and at Castle Drogo.

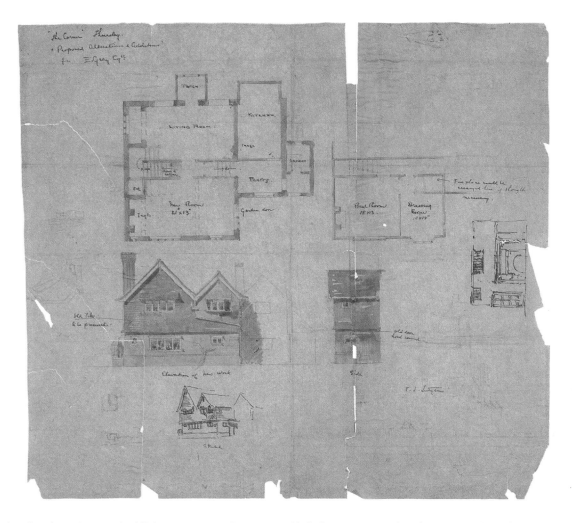

4. Design for alterations and additions to a row of cottages called The Corner, at Thursley, Surrey, for Edmund Gray, 1888

Pencil, coloured wash and pen on brown paper (330 × 395)

This was Lutyens's first executed work, designed in the evenings when he was in the office of Sir Ernest George and Harold Peto. He added a large tile-hung wing to the back of the cottages, very similar in style to Redcote, Harpenden by Ernest George, who greatly influenced Lutyens at this stage of his work.

The designs show the easy informality of his drawing style which well suited his amused contempt for professionalism. This is Lutyens's typical 'letter for the builder', with plans, sketch of the fireplace, elevations and thumb-nail perspective all combined on one sheet.

5. **Preliminary design for Crooksbury House, near Farnham, Surrey, for Arthur Chapman,** *c*1889-91

Pencil and watercolour (205 × 235)

Crooksbury was Lutyens's first building of any size and importance and its commission enabled him to leave Sir Ernest George's office and set up on his own. He later added to the building in three phases – in 1898, 1901-02 and 1914. In watercolour, this perspective was clearly made to 'charm' an important client, as Arthur Chapman – later Sir Arthur – was a Calcutta merchant and Chairman of Surrey County Council. The design is close to what was executed on the south side of the existing west wing, although the first phase of Crooksbury was twice the size of the cottage shown in this drawing.

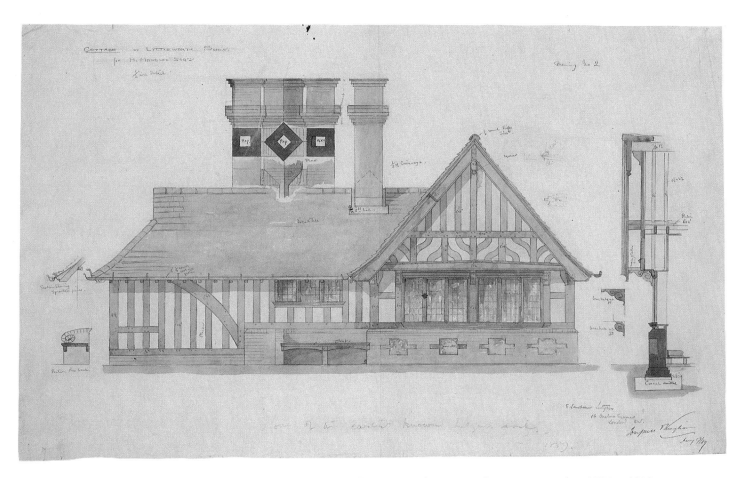

6. **Design for the gardener's cottage at Littleworth Cross, Seale, Surrey, for Harry Mangles, 17 May 1889**

Pencil, coloured wash and pen (450 × 745)

Designed for Mrs Chapman's brother, Harry Mangles, the most famous rhododendron grower of his time, the house is now called Squirrel Hill and survives embedded at one end of a later house *c*1920. Its high Tudor chimney, shown in plan, side and front elevation, and ornamental half-timber work again reflect Sir Ernest George's work. It was at Littleworth Cross that Lutyens first met Gertrude Jekyll in May 1889.

the Gardener's Cottage

7. Designs for the gardener's cottage and The Hut at Munstead Wood, Munstead, Surrey, from the Munstead Wood sketchbook, pp16 verso and 17 recto, c1892-93

Pencil, pen and watercolour, bound in buff cloth covers (125 × 180)

Provenance: Recovered by RA Wood, of the builders J W Falkner Sons Ltd, from rubbish removed from the Lutyens office at 5 Eaton Gate in 1939; presented by RA Wood to Viscountess Ridley (Lutyens's daughter Ursula) in 1956; presented to the RIBA on indefinite loan by the Misses Jane, Susannah and Jessica Ridley, 1983.

Gertrude Jekyll had settled in Munstead with her family at Munstead House (by JJ Stevenson) and carried out horticultural experiments in her woodland estate across the road. This sketchbook shows that she had been thinking about building Munstead Wood on this site for several years before 1895-96, and that the two designs shown on these pages were drawn in 1892-93 and built in 1893-94. Hussey has suggested that the sketchbook was probably compiled when 'the weekend at

Munstead became a habit' and she and Lutyens 'began the witty and exciting sport of working out the designs together' – he perhaps bringing with him or adding fresh sketches on each visit. On the left is a watercolour perspective of the gardener's cottage (p28), built for Miss Jekyll's Swiss gardener, Albert Zumbach, in 1893. On the right is a design for The Hut (p29) inscribed 'Abandoned Oct 9th/1892/Restored to favour July 16/93'. She lived an Arts and Crafts life of comparative simplicity in The Hut while Munstead Wood was being built. Both buildings were exact re-creations of vernacular Surrey cottages: one being tile-hung and half-timbered, the other tile-hung with a hipped roof and corbie-stepped chimney. Both were used as illustrations of local cottages by Miss Jekyll in *Old West Surrey*, 1904.

8. Preliminary design for Munstead Wood, Munstead, Surrey, from the Munstead Wood sketchbook, p6 recto, *c*1893

Pen and watercolour (125 × 180)

The sketchbook is particularly interesting for showing the evolution of the design for Munstead Wood. The drawings show a much larger house, with three chimney stacks and numerous gables and projections, but of seemingly random composition. The emphasis is on its picturesque effect – so brilliantly conveyed in these watercolour sketches which could be by Helen Allingham or Birket Foster rather than an architect. The materials suggested are tile and render, with brick door and window surrounds – later used to good effect at Goddards. Munstead Wood was built of Bargate stone and tile, with oak door and window frames. The forms (eventually much simplified) and general orientation of the house, however, remained the same. As built the principal front faced south to the garden as in this watercolour inscribed 'From the SW'.

9. **Preliminary design for the north front (back), Munstead Wood, Munstead, Surrey, from the Munstead Wood sketchbook, p7 recto, c1893**

Pen and watercolour (125 × 180)

This study for the north front shows a curious single-storey annexe to the north-west corner, with a flat roof terrace and pergola accessible from an octagonal turret. Lutyens has labelled this 'Bad'. The annexe was replaced in the final design by Miss Jekyll's workshop. She admitted in *Home and Garden* (1900), p16, that she had 'made one false start' a year or two before she and her architect started the actual planning of the house, so the early designs in this sketchbook must be seen as the trial run for a house that later made Lutyens's name for its simple and concise composition from local forms and materials.

10. **Design for the dining-room sideboard, Munstead Wood, Munstead, Surrey, from the Munstead Wood sketchbook, p9 recto, c1893**

Pen, pencil and watercolour (125 × 180)

The drawing is interesting for showing how Lutyens so often projected his imagination into the life to be led in his designs; this sideboard was never built but Miss Jekyll did have one rather like it in the dining room at Munstead Wood, laden with her collection of pewter.

11. Preliminary design for the south front, looking towards the summer-house, Munstead Wood, Munstead, Surrey, from the Munstead Wood sketchbook, p6 verso, *c*1893

Pen and watercolour (125 × 180)

The summer-house in this design later became a lean-to porch which concealed the entrance to the front door on the east side.

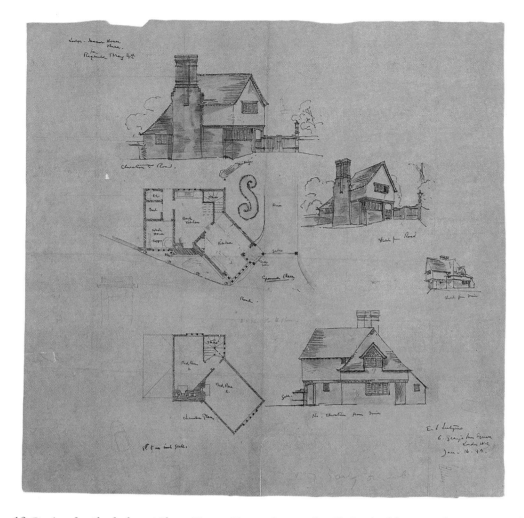

12. **Design for the lodge at Shere Manor House, Surrey, for Sir Reginald Bray, 16 January 1894**

Brown pen and coloured wash (480 × 510)

All the essentials of this clever design for a lodge on a corner site are conveyed on one sheet which gives plans, elevations and perspective 'sketch' from the road. A second thumb-nail sketch of the lodge as seen from the drive is added to give a three-dimensional view of the complete design. This is the earliest surviving drawing signed from Lutyens's first office at No 6 Gray's Inn Square and not from his parents' home at No 16 Onslow Square.

13. Record sketches of Chinthurst Hill, Wonersh, Surrey, *c*mid-1890s

Pen and wash (250 × 200)

Chinthurst Hill was a relatively early scheme designed for Miss Aemilia Guthrie in 1893. Stylistically it is Tudor with inset, Gothic, traceried windows suggesting a medieval manor house altered in Elizabethan times; inside is a Gothic hall and finely detailed open oak staircase. This drawing is not a design but one of several small sheets recording his latest work in the years 1892-94, which he made to send to Herbert Baker in South Africa. Baker had also been in Sir Ernest George's office with Lutyens and both remained good friends until their later 'Bakerloo' in New Delhi; they went on a sketching tour in Wales, Shropshire and Cheshire in September 1890 and corresponded with one another after Baker went to South Africa in 1892.

Porte Fleuviale de Circonstance

14. Design for the entrance to an imaginary palace called 'Château d'Ease, en Air, sur Fleuve des Rêves', in the 'Castle-in-the-Air' sketchbook, p2, *c*1895–96

Pencil and watercolour (125 × 185)

Provenance: As for plate 7.

The sketchbook was drawn to amuse Mrs Robert Webb of Milford House, near Godalming, a great friend from his boyhood who died of cancer in 1897. Bearing inside its cover his symbol for Barbara Webb – a lamb with a halo – it is filled with delicate pencil and watercolour designs for a vast château, accessible only by water, standing on the bank of a river. The main approach, seen in this drawing, was called the 'Porte Fleuviale de Circonstance': a flight of steps, flanked by golden statues of lambs rises to a terrace. A green copper-sheathed

dome is visible above a huge Romanesque portal. The terrace is enclosed by tall pavilions crowned by San Micheli loggias with pink marble columns and arched recesses in their bases like those he introduced into gardens in his later London County Hall design.

Drawn from the Renaissance and Byzantine sources that were inspiring architects during the 1890s, the sketchbook is full of ideas that were expressed much later in Lutyens's designs for the Viceroy's House, the Dublin Bridge and Liverpool Cathedral.

**15. Preliminary design for additions to the Ferry Inn, Rosneath, Dunbartonshire, for HRH Princess Louise,
Duchess of Argyll, March 1896**

Pen and watercolour with pencil (430 × 700)

Lutyens first met Princess Louise, fourth daughter of Queen Victoria, in 1896 and was no doubt flattered by her informal artistic ways and frequent summonses to Kensington Palace. Although he played his inimitable jokey role with the Princess, who was, as he said, 'full of bounce and fun', he was quite ready to produce one of his more finished watercolour designs for such an important client. The new wing, to contain reception rooms and a bar with bedrooms above, is added to the existing modest country inn on the Argyll estate, which is shown on the left of each elevation. This preliminary design shows several rather grand features, for example, the Baroque entrance with segmental pediment and the mannered east elevation with its semicircular windows. It was abandoned later for one that incorporated many more local features. The original inn was demolished in 1960 and the truncated remains of the Lutyens wing are all that now remain.

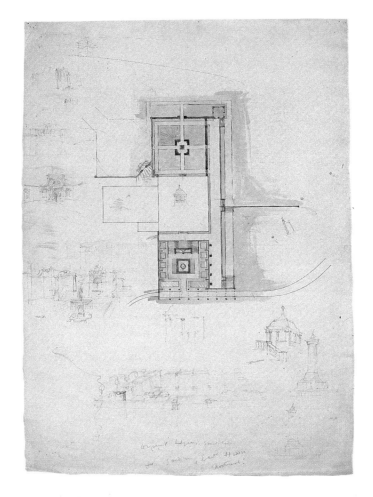

16. Design for a garden and garden features at East Haddon Hall, Northamptonshire, for David Charles Guthrie, 1897

Pencil, pen and coloured wash (565 × 755)

Lutyens designed two square gardens on either side of the eighteenth-century house, which were carried out although little survives today. In one, steps on either side of a niche lead down to a fountain; brick piers on two sides create bays with a pergola at the far end. The other garden has a sun-dial with a gazebo at the end of the terrace nearby. The garden features and layout owe much to the seventeenth-century gardens illustrated in Reginald Blomfield and F Inigo Thomas's *The Formal Garden in England* (1892), which saw the architectural treatment of gardens as 'an extension of the principles of design which govern the house to the grounds which surround it' – a theory often followed by Lutyens, perhaps unconsciously, in his garden work.

17. **Design for a proposed house at Mayville, Le Touquet-Paris-Plage, France, for John Whitley, 1897**

Pencil, pen and coloured crayon (410 × 440)

In the 1890s John Robinson Whitley (1843-1922), a Yorkshire businessman, the founder and organiser of Le Touquet, purchased a tract of land fronting the beach which he named 'Mayville' after Princess, later Queen, Mary and launched Mayville Ltd, which proposed a luxury resort planned on very grand lines. At some point he must have contacted Lutyens for designs, for the architect wrote to Lady Emily on 24 May 1897

'What fun if Mayville comes off. If enough I might start an office there! and put my Emy in charge!' Nothing came of this initial project, however, although Le Touquet prospered later as an English colony. The design and its presentation is pure fantasy with a French touch; Lutyens was using corner oriels at Le Bois des Moutiers at Varengeville in the same year.

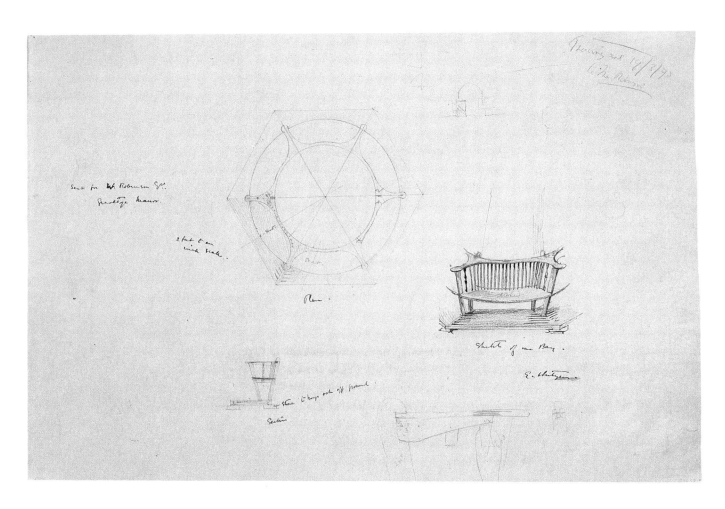

18. Design for a wooden circular seat at Gravetye Manor, Sussex, for William Robinson, 1898

Pen, pencil and brown crayon (380 × 580)

This design for an intriguing circular seat, divided into six bays and resting on an oak platform, doubled-up as a working drawing, as the sheet contains all the details necessary for its construction. As it indicates that a tracing was sent to Mr Robinson on '19/3/1898', it is likely that the design was carried out although the seat does not survive today. Lutyens cultivated Robinson – the author of the classic *The English Flower Garden* (1883) – assiduously in the hope of a job, even though, as he said – 'he bores so'. Nothing came of this until Robinson later commissioned offices for *The Garden* at 42 Kingsway, London, in 1906.

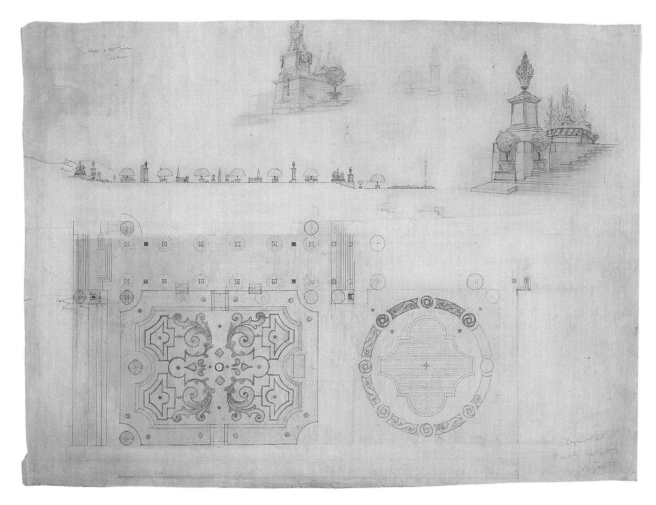

19 **Design for gardens at Eaton Hall, Cheshire, for the Duke of Westminster,** *c* **1897-98**

Pen, pencil and coloured crayon (570 × 780)

The prestigious commission from the Duke of Westminster to design gardens and garden buildings at Eaton Hall probably came to Lutyens through Miss Jekyll, who had been given the job in the 1870s of overseeing the interior furnishings of the Waterhouse building. She did not, however, collaborate with him on the planting of this formal Italian garden layout on the terraces on the east side of the house – a formality which is matched by this finely detailed presentation design. Early *Country Life* photographs from 1901 of the completed scheme show that the design was not executed.

20. Design for the Tea-house sun-dial at Eaton Hall, Cheshire, for the Duke of Westminster, 1898

Pen, pencil and coloured wash (400 × 500)

This design, drawn to the scale of 1 inch to 1 foot, combines plan, elevation and perspective of an elaborate sun-dial with the motto 'They also serve who only stand and wait'. Tracings were sent to Farmer and Brindley, the leading stonemasons, and the executed sun-dial can be seen in a photograph in *Country Life* (20 April 1901) showing it in front of the Tea-house designed by John Douglas. It has since been removed but traces of Lutyens's layout remain.

21. **Preliminary design for the Methodist Chapel at Overstrand, Norfolk, for Lord Battersea, 1897-98**

Pencil and pen on squared paper (285 × 445)

Lord Battersea commissioned Lutyens to build the chapel in July 1897 and this preliminary sketch explores all the principal elements of the design on one sheet. A simple and ingenious building – Lutyens's first ecclesiastical work – it is built of brick with a round-arched entrance door and a clerestory with lunette windows. Tie beams, which brace the structure, are supported on short, straight buttresses.

In 1899, on 4 August, Lady Emily wrote from Booton Rectory in Norfolk, where she was staying with the amateur architect the Reverend Whitwell Elwin: 'They like your chapel. Fountain [also an architect] says it's very Dutch and he says it is the best ventilated church he has ever seen. I am longing to see it.' Lutyens replied on 7 August: 'It is no use looking at the Overstrand Chapel, it cost $2\frac{1}{2}$ d and is not Dutch or anything at all just a brick wall and a skylight and a door and a stove. The inside spoilt – as its one salvation was simplicity – by a d-d moulding and horrid E[lectric] light fittings. So long as they can make a noise in it, no one else cares for aught else.'

22. Design for Deanery Garden, Sonning, Berkshire, for Edward Hudson, 1899

Pencil, pen and coloured wash (545 × 750)

Lutyens's drawing style in this presentation design is almost purposely naive – something to charm the client, in this case, Edward Hudson, 'dear Huddy', the proprietor of *Country Life*, who was to do more than anyone to promote Lutyens's work in his magazine. The design is quite close to the built work and is assembled like a children's book illustration with a contrasting pair of worm's-eye and bird's-eye perspectives arranged above the sections below. From left to right the sections show the dining-room sideboard and hall fireplace; the bay window and west side of the hall; and a cross section and interior perspective of the first-floor corridor. Weaver called Deanery Garden Lutyens's 'last important essay in half-timber work', which is well conveyed in the finely drawn plain oak beams, pegging and panelling.

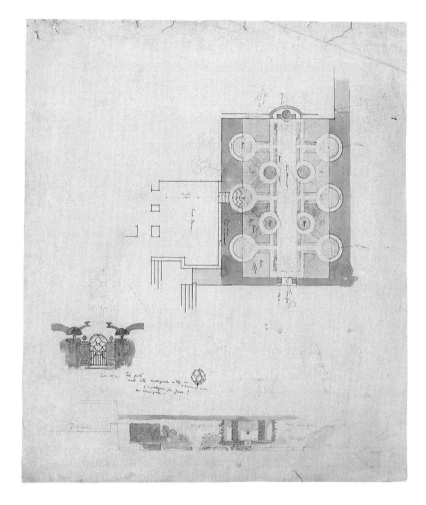

23. Design for the sunken Dutch Garden Court at Orchards, Munstead, Surrey, for Sir William and Lady Chance, *c*1899

Pencil, pen, red pen and coloured wash (570 × 495)

The Dutch Garden at Orchards is, in effect, an outside room and an early exercise in geometry. As the plan shows, York stone loops enclose circles of planting or brick which flank a stone pavement. The garden is enclosed to the east and west by high yew hedges with semicircular bays and seats. On the north is an old stone wall in the middle of which is a curved recess supported by tile-built piers and containing a basin into which water pours from a bronze lion head, the work of Lady Chance. To the south is the gate. The drawing is carefully detailed and defined in red and black pen, with intriguing vignettes. For example, the gateway is inscribed 'Tile posts/ with tile multigonals on top – a cement core/and apologies for yews!! an iron gate'.

24. Preliminary design for Marshcourt, Stockbridge, Hampshire, for Herbert Johnson, *c*1901

Pencil and coloured crayon (535 × 725)

These preliminary designs for the north and south elevations show a heavy thatched roof and 'clunch' walls. As built, the house followed the general disposition of forms in this design and retained much of its vernacular character, particularly on the north front, but it was not thatched and with added bays, parapets and twisted brick chimneys came to assume the appearance of a great Tudor hunting lodge.

Coloured crayon, increasingly used by Lutyens instead of watercolour after 1900, helps to convey the nature of the proposed materials.

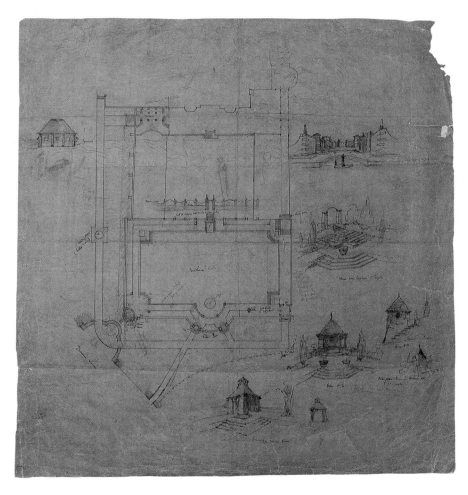

25. Presentation design for the garden, with its garden buildings, at Abbotswood, Stow-on-the-Wold, Gloucestershire, for Mark Fenwick, 1901

Pen and coloured crayon on tracing paper (760 × 750)

Lutyens was introduced by Gertrude Jekyll to Mark Fenwick, a banker and amateur gardener. He carried out alterations to the existing building as well as designing the elaborate terraced garden on the south side of the house. Steps from a terrace first lead down to a paved flower garden with a pergola on the east which is now demolished. Further steps then lead down to the new tennis lawn with its central, semicircular viewpoint and corner pavilions, the whole enclosed by a retaining wall. This design illustrates each interesting feature with perspective vignettes, giving three different views, for example, of the west summer-house. The central viewpoint and the east summer-house were not realised.

28. Design for a beach estate at Rossall, Lancashire, for TB Lumb, 1901

Pen and crayon on brown paper (445 × 680)

An exciting commission, which eventually petered out, was the proposal to lay out a seaside garden village at Rossall Beach. Lutyens described it as 'my new Town' and estimated that the shell would cost about £400,000; he would receive £100 for sketches and 2½ per cent on general building except for the church, hotel and public buildings seen in this bird's-eye perspective. Only one of Lutyens's houses was built in Cross Way, together with the lodges of Way Gate with four adjacent cottages. The layout and design, however, did prefigure his work at Hampstead Garden Suburb.

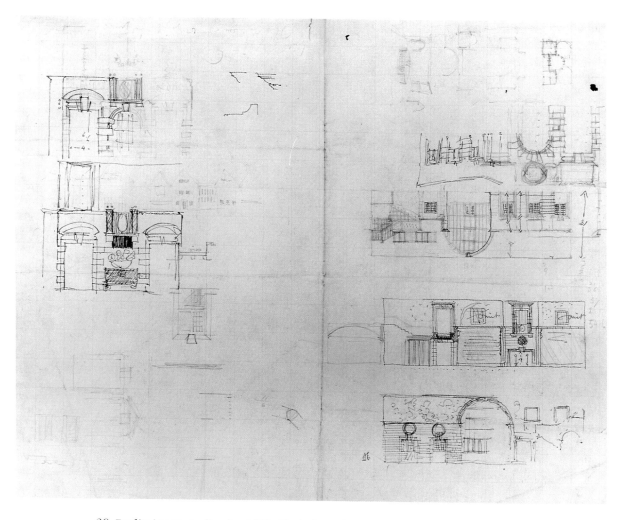

29. **Preliminary studies for Little Thakeham, Sussex, for Ernest Blackburn, 1902**

Pencil and pen on squared paper (430 × 560)

Built for Ernest Blackburn, an amateur gardener, Little Thakeham takes the form of a traditional Tudor manor house with a great classical hall. The hall is a large double-height space divided by a screen with paired doorways, their surrounds are taken from Batty Langley's *City and Country Builder's and Workman's Treasury of Designs* (1740), Lutyens's office bible.

On the left of the sheet are alternative elevations of the screen wall and a thumb-nail sketch of the garden elevation; on the right are elevations of the fireplace and window walls of the hall, and above, upside-down, an elevation with sketch perspective below of the window wall as executed and an alternative design for the screen wall.

30. **Preliminary design for St John's Institute, Tufton Street, London, for Archdeacon Wilberforce, 1902**

Pencil, crayon and pen (280 × 260)

The Institute was built as a parish hall for St John's Church, Smith Square, of which Archdeacon Wilberforce, a friend of Lutyens's parents, was rector. The design took some time to evolve, from 1899-1905, and the built version, with its three plain Wren arches to the street and five simple windows without pediments, differs from this early exercise on the theme of a Palladian town house. The drawing is dated 'MCMII' and is Lutyens's earliest attempt at street architecture. It required 'hard thought', and several changes in design. He admitted in April 1905 that he was 'struggling on Tufton Street'.

_31._ Design for a house on the Hudson River, New York, for Mr EH Harriman, 1903

Pen and wash on tracing paper (165 × 305)

Harriman, a railway millionaire and the uncle of the statesman Averell Harriman, had already commissioned competing designs from half a dozen American architects when in 1903, on the advice of Sir Austin Lee, he suggested that Lutyens send one in too. In a letter dated 10 August 1903, Lutyens told Lady Emily: 'This morning I called on Mr Harriman the multimillionaire. I am to make sketches for a house – money no object!! Whether I get it or no is another matter – all America is after the job . . .

the site is a very difficult one all rock 22,000 acres he has . . .' The project produced one of Lutyens's early monumental designs – a Renaissance palazzo, the low viewpoint in the drawing exaggerating the scale of the house. He was not successful; Mrs Harriman had hinted that her husband had said 'it was a bad beginning to start with an English architect'. The New York architects, Carrère and Hastings, won the commission instead and built Arden House (1905-10), which still survives.

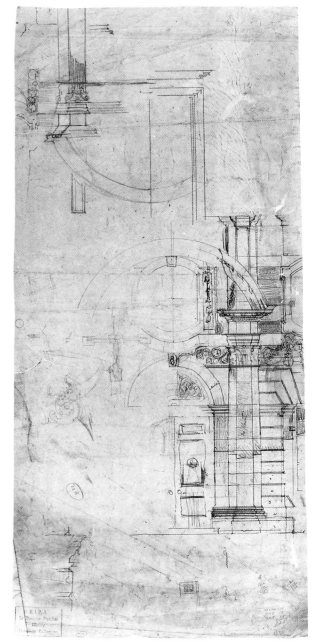

32. **Preliminary design for the entrance door of the**
Country Life **offices, Nos 2-10 Tavistock Street, London,**
for Edward Hudson, 1904

Pencil and pen on oiled tracing paper (750 × 355)

The *Country Life* building was Lutyens's first executed London
work and an early example of his Hampton Court 'Wrenaissance'
style. The focus of the design is centred on the elaborate
entrance doorway with its segmental pediment and decoration
carved by Abraham Broadbent in the manner of Grinling Gibbons. Lutyens later wrote, on 4 February 1905, that 'as a work
of art Versailles cannot be compared with our Hampton Court.
This for a firm belief is very comforting.'

33. **Preliminary study for a hotel at Hardelot-Plage, Pas de Calais, France, for John Whitley, 1905**

Pencil and crayon on squared paper (445 × 750)

After Le Touquet (plate 17), Whitley had turned his attention to developing Hardelot, south of Boulogne, as a sister 'Pleasaunce', and had asked Lutyens to design a hotel. It took the form – as this worm's-eye view shows – of a medieval château (very much in keeping with the character of local châteaux in the Pas de Calais area with their round brick towers), with a square central hall over a hydro which has corridors radiating from it to the main rooms arranged in a diamond configuration. Rooms indicated are 'Big Di/Small Di/Billia[rd]/Writing Rm/Ladies . . . Big hall over Hydro/Water Tower' and '100 beds'. It seemed to please Whitley for Lutyens wrote to Lady Emily on 13 September 1905: 'I have received a letter from Whitley – Hardelot you remember – saying the plan was a huge success and that he wanted two hotels!' However, despite seeing 'some Frenchmen' in London in April the following year, nothing came of the project.

55

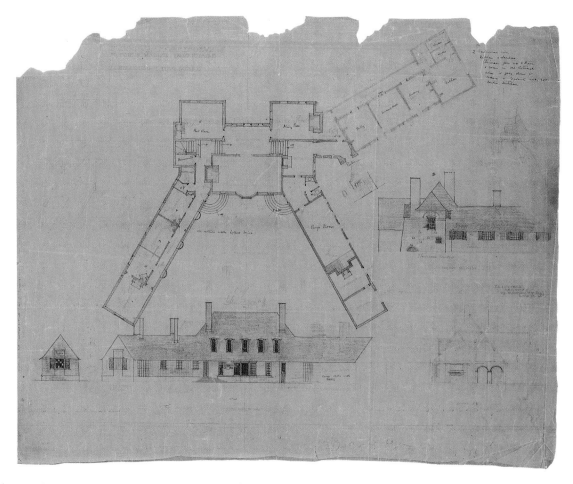

34. Design for Clos du Dan at Varengeville, near Dieppe, France, for M Guillaume Mallet, 1905

Pencil and coloured crayon on tracing paper (650 × 790)

Very little is known about this project. According to Robert Mallet (January 1994), however, Le Clos du Dan is a farmhouse opposite the main entrance to Le Bois des Moutiers. In 1905 Guillaume proposed to alter and enlarge it as a residence for his daughter Pascaline and asked Lutyens to propose a scheme. Nothing came of it and later Lutyens persuaded him to build a completely new house – Les Communes.

35. **Design for alterations to Ashby St Ledger's, Northamptonshire, for the Hon Ivor Guest (later first Viscount Wimborne), *c*1904**

Pen and watercolour (535 × 1010)

This delicate pen and watercolour elevation shows the east, garden front of the house with Lutyens's first proposals for alterations, which were not executed until 1909/10.

The drawing can be read from left to right. First is the church, then the entrance buildings; the original 1652 Jacobean bay; Lutyens's proposed remodelling of the house restoring the central wall with its square bay and north-east corner bay and gable; his proposed additions to the north, which were changed in 1909 by the addition of the north hall and adjoining timber-framed, seventeenth-century house transported from Ipswich; and finally gates, a farm building and bridge, designed by Lutyens but not as executed. The drawing is clever in suggesting the rightness of the new additions and could almost be a topographical sketch of old work.

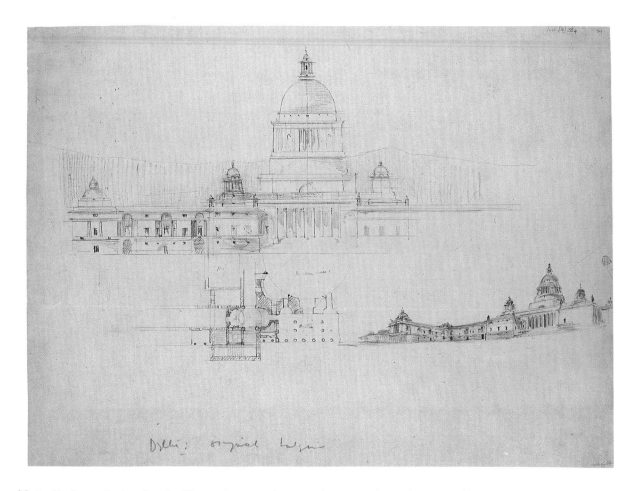

38. **Preliminary design for the Viceroy's House (now Rashtrapati Bhavan), New Delhi, India, *c*late 1912-early 1913**

Pencil, pen and coloured crayon (465 × 630)

The transfer of the seat of government of British India from Calcutta to Delhi was proclaimed by George V at the Delhi Coronation Durbar in 1911. Lutyens was invited to join the Delhi Planning Commission in January 1912 – leaving for India on 1 April 1912. Between the end of April and early the following year, when he was officially appointed architect to the Viceroy's House, he worked on a series of designs which were constantly revised and then finalised during 1913-14.

This early design, with its High Renaissance dome and Palladian windows, must pre-date a letter Lutyens wrote to the Viceroy on 9 March 1913: 'I think the dome will look better without a cupola on the top; it will look less ecclesiastical and more in sympathy with the domes of India, and give a paramount position to the flag staff.'

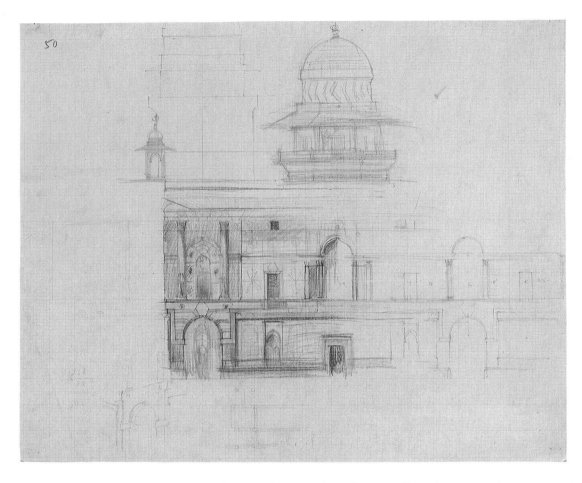

39. **Preliminary design for the Viceroy's House (now Rashtrapati Bhavan), New Delhi, India,** *c.* **December 1912-March 1913**

Pencil, pen and coloured crayon on squared paper (430 × 545)

From the start Lutyens had believed in an ordered, monumental architecture for New Delhi based on the logic of the classical tradition. But both the King and the Viceroy favoured the Indian style, which Lutyens at first reacted against strongly. The Viceroy, however, was persuaded by his designs of late 1912 and by a sense of compromise in Lutyens's attitude that suggested he was capable of the synthesis aspired to by British policy in India. The Viceroy recommended Lutyens's appointment on 7 January 1913.

This sketch is one of the few that survive which shows Lutyens exploring the use of Indian motifs, and may have been made during his second visit to India when he was sent off to see Agra, Fatehpur-Sikri, Mandu and other ancient sites. It shows the *chattri*, the small Indian roof pavilion, and the *chujja*, the projecting stone cornice – both of which were incorporated into the Viceroy's House – as well as the application of the pointed arch to a Palladian window.

40. Preliminary design for the Viceroy's House (now Rashtrapati Bhavan), New Delhi, India, *c*March 1913-14

Pencil, pen and coloured crayon on squared paper (430 × 545)

This sketch is closer to the final design. The Palladian windows and High Renaissance dome have gone, to be replaced by a lower, more Indian dome, roof-top fountains, *chujjas* and the final rhythm of solids and voids along the elevations. It is one of seventy-four surviving early studies for the Viceroy's House at the RIBA, all made on the familiar pad of graph paper.

62

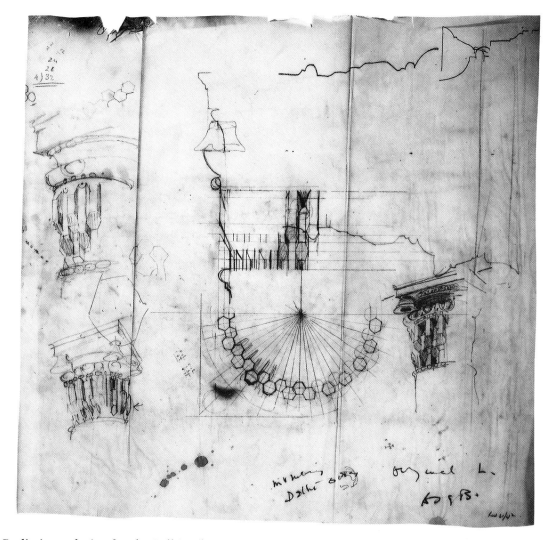

41. **Preliminary design for the Delhi order, Viceroy's House (Rashtrapati Bhavan), New Delhi, India, *c*1914**

Pencil on tracing paper (665 × 740)

Lutyens invented his own order for the Viceroy's House, which he later re-used in many of his designs, notably at the British Embassy in Washington, at Middleton Park and in his Liverpool Cathedral design. In London it can be seen on the facade of No 120 Pall Mall. The capital consists of a studded and corrugated neck supporting a flat abacus with bells – the bells set in stone so that they cannot sound the downfall of a dynasty.

42. Design for an art gallery taking the form of a bridge across the River Liffey, Dublin, for the Corporation of Dublin, 1913

Pen, watercolour and crayon, detail, (330 × 605)

The controversy over a suitable site for a gallery to house Sir Hugh Lane's collection of paintings still survives today. Lane had originally lent his collection to a temporary Municipal Gallery in Dublin in 1906, stipulating that a permanent building be erected in a few years. He then met up with Lutyens in about 1910 and they became good friends; he had recommended him to design the Johannesburg Art Gallery and believed in his abilities. 'He is a walking advertisement for me', as Lutyens said in 1910. In 1912 he asked Lutyens to design his Dublin gallery, first on a site on St Stephen's Green, and then, because there was no other suitable place in the city, on a bridge across the Liffey. The bridge scheme took the form of the letter 'H' in plan. The down strokes represent the two main galleries, one on either quay, and the cross stroke a minor connecting gallery surmounted by an open colonnaded footbridge. It is a bridge building rather than a means of passage across water and evoked the spirit of the Rialto bridge and the Pulteney bridge at Bath. Unfortunately, the Dublin Corporation neither had the money, nor, in spite of a tireless campaign by WB Yeats in support of Lutyens's design, were they prepared to appoint an English architect.

43. **Preliminary design for the church of St Jude-on-the-Hill, Hampstead Garden Suburb, Barnet, for the Hampstead Garden Suburb Trust, *c*1909**

Pencil and coloured crayon (750 × 875)

This is one of fifteen designs for successive preliminary schemes, many of which did not find favour with Mrs Henrietta Barnet because of their height and scale. This design, however, is close to what was built except for the lower west end, which was reduced, and the clerestory windows which were omitted.

St Jude's is set within the Central Square with the Institute on the left; there are also sections of the church and interior perspectives. Lutyens wrote to Lady Emily on 12 October 1909: 'Mrs Barnet was vanquished and the church reduced, is agreed to, but oh I do want more money for *my* church . . .'

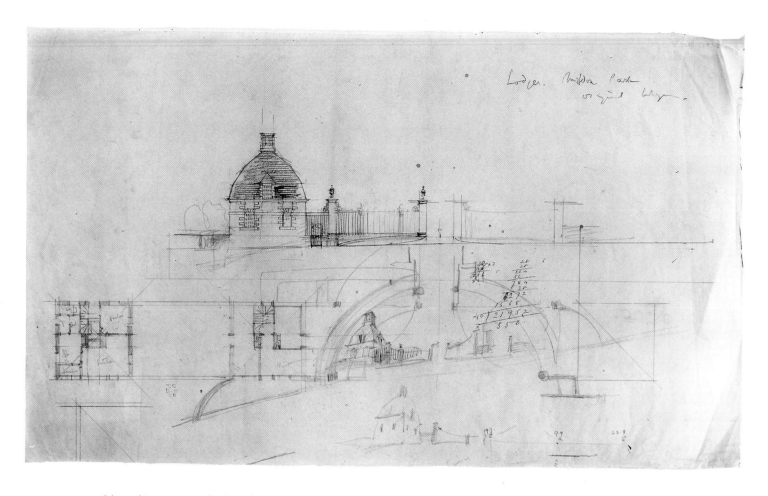

44. **Preliminary study for a lodge and gates at Meldon Park, Northumberland, for Colonel Cookson, 1909**

Pencil, crayon and pen (480 × 840)

In July 1908 Lutyens met the owners of Meldon Park who had just come into a fortune and wanted him to build them new gates and a lodge. This study shows him simultaneously working out the design in plan, elevation and perspective – a design that has both elegance and a satisfying geometry. A semicircular forecourt leads to the entrance gates; on the left is the lodge, its facade forming the edge of the park wall. The lodge is an exact square with a Mansard pyramidal roof, four dormers and a central chimney-stack. The ground-floor plan is on the far left with parlour, kitchen, back kitchen, larder, fuel and WC. The bedroom plan is below the elevation.

The presentation design in Lutyens's hand is also at the RIBA, dated 9 February, and hardly varies from the earlier study. Nothing came of this scheme although Lutyens did carry out alterations to the main staircase and hall of this house by Dobson between the Wars.

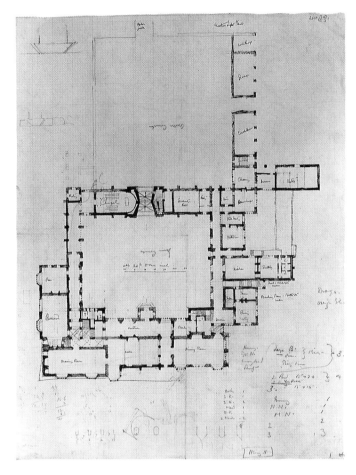

45. Preliminary design for Castle Drogo, Drewsteignton, Devon, for Julius C Drewe, 1910

Pencil and pen on squared paper (545 × 430)

Drogo was built for Julius Drewe, founder of the Home and Colonial Stores, who had first approached Lutyens in late 1909 to build him the kind of castle that might have belonged to his thirteenth-century ancestor, Drogo de Teynton. Lutyens began working up the first rough sketches on a voyage to South Africa in November 1910, and finalised the first scheme in the following April. This sketch plan shows the first asymmetrical courtyard design of enormous scale with inner and outer courts, great hall and chapel. The sketch is typical of hundreds he made throughout his career on a squared graph pad, which he used in the office, and which travelled with him to India and South Africa.

46. **Preliminary design for Castle Drogo, Drewsteignton, Devon, for Julius C Drewe, *c*1910**

Pencil on squared paper (430 × 545), detail

These early sketches would have added life to the first asymmetrical courtyard design. They show elevations of the courts and an interior perspective of the great hall; on the left is the coach house gateway.

47. **Preliminary design for Castle Drogo, Drewsteignton, Devon, for Julius C Drewe, 1911**

Pencil, pen and coloured crayon on squared paper (405 × 530)

The design developed through a series of courtyard schemes. This presentation design, with added crayon, is clearly intended for the client and shows what Peter Inskip has called 'the U-shaped courtyard scheme', datable to 1911. The perspective sketch on the right and the lower elevation show the south-facing range, which included the great hall, shown here with three Gothic traceried windows between buttresses which Lutyens first used on the entrance front of his prize-winning country house design of 1888 (plate 3).

69

48. Design for Castle Drogo, Drewsteignton, Devon, for Julius C Drewe, *c*1920

Pencil, pen and coloured crayon on No 17 Queen Anne's Gate writing paper (205 × 255)

In 1912 the size of the house was arbitrarily reduced by half because the family at last decided that the building on which construction had already started was much larger than was needed. Then after the War the design was even further re-duced leaving only a narrow south end and an east-facing house. This sketch, which is close to the building as executed, shows a view of the castle from the south-west. The office moved in the autumn of 1910 to No 17 Queen Anne's Gate.

49. **Design for Castle Drogo, Drewsteignton, Devon, for Julius C Drewe, *c*1920**

Pen, pencil and coloured crayon on No 17 Queen Anne's Gate writing paper (205 × 255)

A perspective of the south and east sides of the castle, showing the sharp fins of the south end and the 'elemental' qualities of Lutyens's castle architecture. The drawing is inscribed 'Return JCW/Castle Drogo'; JC Walker was the indispensable clerk of works at Drogo who would have drawn up many of Lutyens's sketches to scale in an office on site.

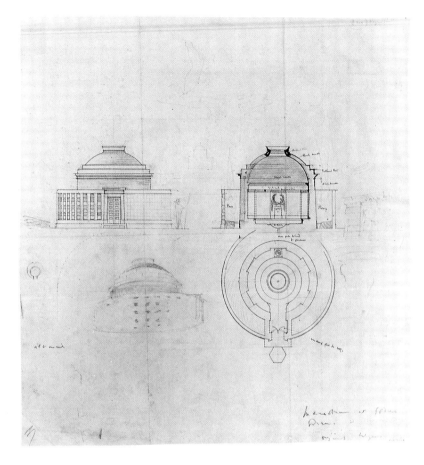

50. Design for a mausoleum for the Philipson family, Golders Green Crematorium, Barnet, 1914

Brown pen and coloured crayon on detail paper (700 × 665)

Apart from a few gravestones for his family and friends, Lutyens only designed two mausolea before the end of the First World War. The first was the Hannen columbarium in Wargrave Churchyard (1905), and the second the Philipson Mausoleum. Both have a Roman character, the latter especially evoking a miniature Pantheon surrounded by a grille-like wall. The Philipson mausoleum still survives and is important in prefiguring his work on the later war memorials.

51. **Preliminary design for offices for the *Daily Chronicle* on the corner of Fleet Street and Salisbury Court, London, for United Newspapers Ltd, 1914**

Pencil and blue crayon (400 × 760)

Lutyens often conceived a building as a sculptor might – in terms of solids and voids, rather than in terms of construction – as this study clearly shows.

The scheme was never realised, owing to the outbreak of the First World War, but Lutyens later built the Reuter's building on the same site.

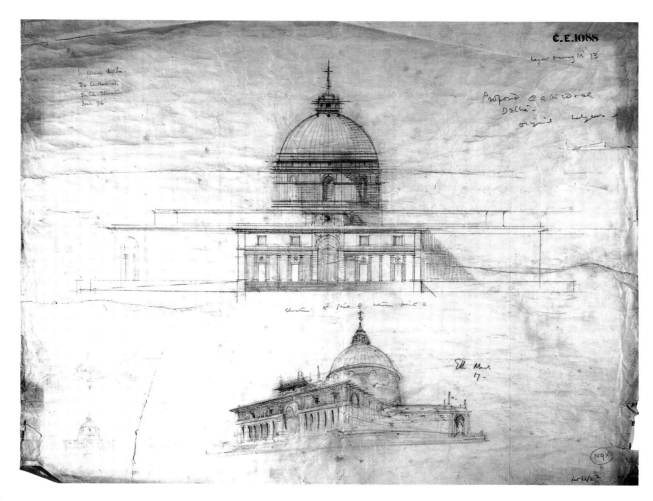

52. **Preliminary design for a proposed Anglican Cathedral at New Delhi, India, 1917**

Pencil and crayon on detail paper (580 × 760)

Lutyens's scheme for a cathedral – or 'big church' as he called it – was sited on a hexagonal site at the south end of Queen's Way, but was never executed. He fought hard for a non-Gothic design as this drawing shows – his building taking the form of a centrally planned church with three radiating wings.

This sketch elevation and perspective show entrance steps leading up to the open, columnar narthex with overhanging chujjas and a great dome behind. The low viewpoint in the perspective underscores the intended monumentality of the design.

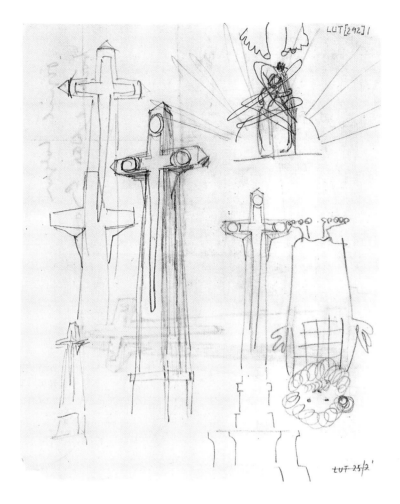

53. **Preliminary studies for the War Cross, for the Imperial War Graves Commission, early 1918**

Pencil on writing paper (255 × 205)

Lutyens and Reginald Blomfield both designed memorial crosses, although Blomfield's more conventionally Christian, sword-bearing, Cross of Sacrifice was almost everywhere preferred and was most often used in conjunction with Lutyens's non-denominational Stone of Remembrance.

Lutyens based his design for the cross on the Celtic type with its less overtly Calvary shape. These rough studies show crosses of this type but also show swords and bosses which were not included in the final reduced and spare design. Celtic crosses, and modern examples of the same type by Sir Robert Lorimer and other architects, were illustrated in Lawrence Weaver's *Memorials and Monuments* (1915) which Lutyens would have known well. Good examples of his War Cross can be found at Wargrave in Berkshire and in Busbridge Churchyard, Surrey.

54. Preliminary study for a proposed temporary war shrine in Hyde Park, London, mid-1918

Pencil and pen on squared paper (580 x 450), detail

A temporary war shrine (but not by Lutyens) was erected in Hyde Park on the fourth anniversary of the outbreak of the First World War. Its wide appeal prompted Sir Alfred Mond, First Commissioner of Works, to ask Lutyens to produce a more fitting monument for which SJ Waring (of Waring and Gillow) was prepared to pay. Its actual construction, however, was made unnecessary by the decision in 1919 to build the Cenotaph.

This drawing is one of ten surviving preliminary sheets showing a scheme of monumental size, with a great entrance arch leading into a pillared hall behind which are four colonnaded courts. His final scheme was far more modest and consisted of a monolithic stone altar (the Great War Stone) raised on a stepped platform, flanked by pylons.

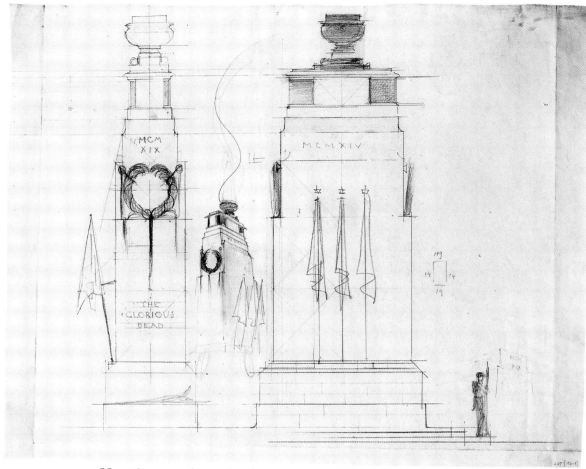

55. Preliminary design for the Cenotaph in Whitehall, London, July 1919

Pencil and crayon (685 × 1015), detail

Lloyd George saw Lutyens early in June 1919 and told him a 'catafalque' was needed as a temporary structure to form a focus for the Peace Celebrations to be held on 19 July.

The executed design is represented in what is thought to be the original first sketch, dated '4.6.19', now at the Imperial War Museum. On 7 July Lutyens told Lady Emily that Lord Curzon approved his design 'but wanted it less catafalque, so I am putting a basin on it – to spout a pillar of flame by night, and I hope, smoke by day'. This second design is represented in this drawing, made at his drawing board.

The final design, reverted to his original first idea. The temporary Cenotaph, of wood and plaster, was taken down in January 1920 and was replaced by the permanent stone structure, which was unveiled on 11 November 1920, the second anniversary of the Armistice.

56. Preliminary design for the Cenotaph in Whitehall, London, 1919

Pencil and crayon on oiled paper (565 × 705)

Lutyens had originally wanted to use painted stone flags on the permanent structure but had to compromise by having real flags of silk instead. He wrote on 10 August 1920: 'I met Lord Curzon in the street. He was very sympathetic about the flags in silk instead of stone. He says when they blow away and look wretched, as they will, apply to the Cabinet again. He does not realise it will mean rebuilding the Cenotaph.' Lutyens did, however, use stone flags on the twin cenotaphs at Etaples Military Cemetery in France, built at the same time as the Cenotaph.

57. **Design for the All-India War Memorial Arch, New Delhi, India, 1920**

Pencil and coloured crayon on tracing paper (465 × 475)

The memorial arch commemorates the 70,000 Indians who died in the First World War and is sited at the eastern end of the King's Way on a direct axis with the Viceroy's House. A war memorial of some kind was first proposed in 1917 and Lutyens fought hard for a single, symbolic idea instead of a monument that might serve some utilitarian purpose, writing: 'to commemorate this great war a structure should be erected where, independent of creed and caste, all India may commemorate her great men, who have served their King, Emperor and country, now and for all time.' This early struggle for a single, big idea did much to influence the Imperial War Graves Commission in their choice of Memorials for the Missing in the 1920s.

The drawing, dated 'Jan-March 1920', is an early presentation design, emphasising the massive silhouette of the arch set against the rays of the sun. The scheme was approved in 1920, begun in 1921 and dedicated in 1931. The steps and flanking pavilions were not executed.

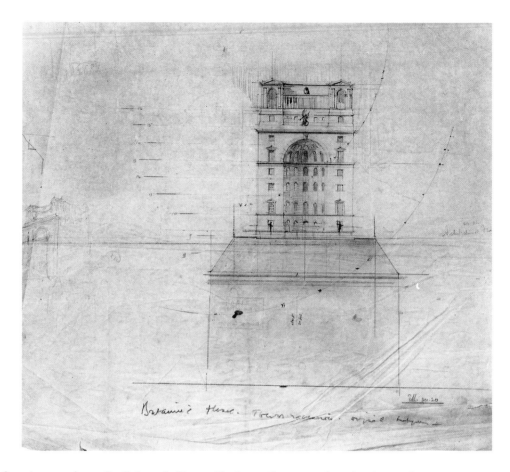

58. Design for a tower scheme for Britannic House, Finsbury Circus, London, for the Anglo-Persian Oil Company, 1920

Pencil and sepia pen on detail paper (635 × 570), detail

Lutyens first received the commission to design Britannic House – his first commercial building in the City – in late 1920. It was a welcome one; in spite of his success with Delhi, he had an overdraft of over £6,000 and in a letter of 2 September 1921 wrote of the 'aching anxiety of these past few years'.

This project, signed and dated 'ELL Dec 20', shows his proposed scheme with a tower which doubled the height of the building to 221 feet above street level. The tower is intricately classical, with a concave hemicycle front with a semi-dome, based on the Giardino della Pigna in the Vatican, and a convex back. Twin symmetrical aedicules form the top storey.

At that time, however, the 1894 Building Act forbade the construction of buildings over 100 feet. Lutyens, perhaps naively, or perhaps thinking he had discovered a planning loophole, suggested that the tower be treated as an 'architectural feature', as if it were a spire or high parapet. But the planners saw – possibly rightly – that the tower was intended as offices for commercial purposes, and formally turned it down in September 1921. A lower Britannic House went ahead measuring 97 feet 9½ inches above pavement level.

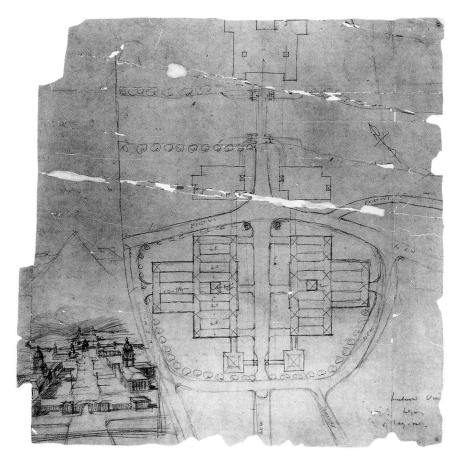

59. Design for a proposed university at Lucknow, India, *c* 1920-21

Pencil on tracing paper (695 × 710)

In April 1920 Lutyens was excited to receive a telegram from Sir Harcourt Butler, Governor of the United Provinces, inviting him to submit designs for a new university. He felt there was some reality in the project – particularly as he had a 'very understanding Chief' in Butler. He worked on the studies and finished designs in late 1920 and January 1921 and they were actually approved. In January 1922, however, he wrote home that 'they have so far negatived the building project and want to add bits of hostels etc to existing buildings'. By December 1922 he told Lady Emily that 'The Lucknow University is off!' Costs obviously played an important part in rejecting this immensely monumental scheme, which, as this plan and bird's-eye perspective shows, certainly evoked Wren's Greenwich and far exceeded it in scale. Lutyens despaired over losing this job, writing later on 24 July 1928: 'What was designed for Lucknow is no use for another site and I want to revive in India a classical tradition such as the Greeks gave her and by which she so greatly profited.'

60. **Design for a proposed university at Lucknow, India,** *c* **1920-21**

Pencil on tracing paper (620 × 850)

This monumental building terminated the main vista in Lutyens's axial plan for the university. It has been likened to the extensive Roman complex at Palestrina, where a series of terraces rose high above the ancient town of Praeneste.

61. Design for Queen Mary's Dolls' House, 1921

Pencil, crayon and pen on detail paper (585 × 1055), detail

The suggestion for the Dolls' House had come, as Mary Lutyens describes, at a luncheon party given by Sir Herbert Morgan in 1920 at which Princess Marie-Louise, a granddaughter of Queen Victoria and EV Lucas had been present as well as Lutyens. The idea was to create for posterity a record of the way of life of a rich English gentleman in 1920 and to present it to Queen Mary as a gesture of good will. The House eventually, however, turned into a small palace for the King and Queen rather than a house for one of their subjects. It was Lutyens who designed it and oversaw its construction in his office, as well as co-

ordinating the sixty artists and two hundred and fifty craftsmen.

The design shows the exterior elevations of the House which stands on a base containing drawers for dolls, the machinery – the electrical transformers, switches, tank, wine cellar, and storeroom – as well as the garage and garden designed by Miss Jekyll. It is inscribed with the 'Dedication/ Presented to the Queen/ by Sir Herbert Morgan/ and some others who/ wish to promote the/ greater by the less' and '7 Apple Tree Yard', Lutyens's Delhi office where the Dolls' House was built. It is now at Windsor Castle.

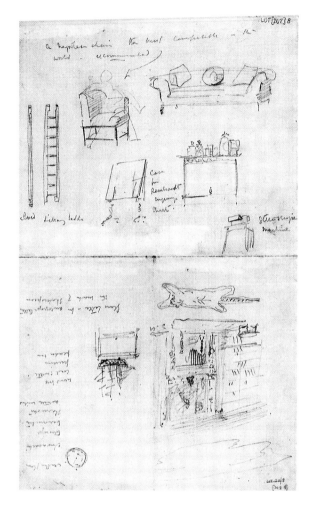

62. Rough studies for the library furniture in Queen Mary's Dolls' House, c1921

Pencil on squared paper (275 × 440)

Lutyens also designed many of the pieces of furniture for the Dolls' House, several of which are miniatures of his own executed designs. In this drawing are, for example, library steps in the form of a cylinder (now at Blagdon); his version of the traditional Napoleon chair inscribed 'the most comfortable in the/world – recommended' (examples at the Victoria and Albert Museum and elsewhere); a sofa; a 'Case for Rembrandt/engravings & charts'; a drinks table with decanters and soda; a 'stereoscope/machine'; and (reversed): the library fireplace and leopard-skin rug; a 'weather glass' and a model of a ship.

84

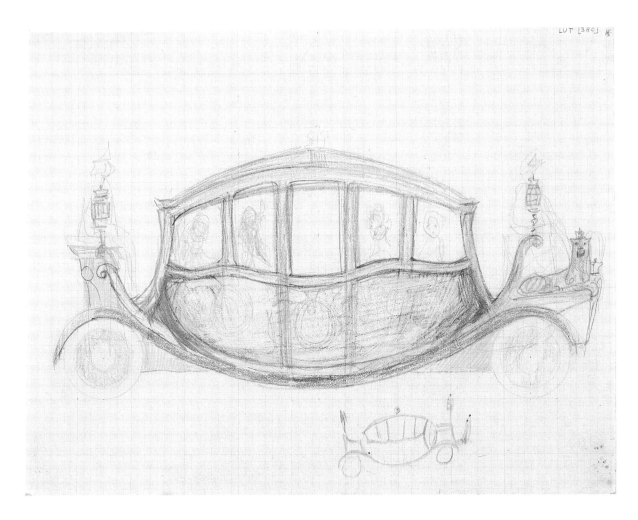

63. Design for a royal state-limousine, *c*1921-24

Pencil and coloured crayon on squared paper (220 × 280)

This design may have been made to accompany Queen Mary's Dolls' House although its garage was eventually filled with models of a seven-seater Rolls-Royce, two Daimlers, a Lanchester saloon, a Vauxhall saloon and a Sunbeam open tourer.

It is one of hundreds of drawings – 'vivreations' – made to amuse his family, friends and potential clients. The drawings,

the famous ones incorporating P & O letter headings, or the transparencies, with themes like 'Crippen in bed' which you held up to the light to see pieces of the victim in a nearby chest of drawers, all helped Lutyens to communicate with his clients, or the wives of clients! Often they were replaced – at dinner – with creative sketches of future projects.

64. **Design for the Midland Bank at No 196a Piccadilly, Westminster, London, 1922**

Pencil, pen and brown crayon (345 × 380)

In 1921 the Midland Bank acquired the site of the old vestry hall at St James's, Piccadilly, and Lutyens's help was sought in providing a suitably tactful replacement next to Wren's church. He produced one of his most successful 'Wrenaissance' designs: an exact square, dressy in the Wren sense and echoing the church in its rusticated quoins.

This was Lutyens's first collaboration with architects who specialised in the planning and construction of this type of building. Lutyens was responsible for the elevations and ground floor ceiling and Whinney, Son and Austen Hall managed the project and carried out all the remaining design work.

65. **Preliminary design for the Memorial to the Missing at St Quentin, Nord, France, for the Imperial War Graves Commission, 1923**

Pencil and coloured crayon on detail paper (700 × 1030)

Because so many casualties in the First World War were uncommemorated – there were 517,000 Missing, whose bodies were never found – the War Commission decided to carve their names on a series of large monuments. One of the first of these was that designed by Lutyens for St Quentin in 1923 and approved 'with acclamation' in early December 1924. Later, the French were disquieted by the number and scale of these Memorials so the St Quentin Arch was abandoned and the large Memorial for the Missing on the Somme at Thiepval was given to Lutyens instead.

Lutyens's idea of complex interlocking triumphal arches was fully explored – as can be seen in this drawing – in his St Quentin design and was later adapted, with alterations, for the Thiepval Memorial in 1927.

From Sir Edwin L. LUTYENS, R.A.

Telephone No. Victoria 4129,

Telegraphic Address:
"Aedificavi, London."

17, QUEEN ANNE'S GATE,
WESTMINSTER, S.W. 1.

66. A record sketch of the design for the Memorial to the Missing at St Quentin, Nord, France, *c* 1923

Pen and red crayon on No 17 Queen Anne's Gate writing paper (255 × 205)

This sketch was attributed by ASG Butler to the Thiepval scheme but was originally pasted onto another finished design at the RIBA inscribed 'Memorial to the Missing at St Quentin' and dated 'Aug 23'. The sketch differs from the Thiepval design in showing the top of the monument as domed and is very close to the model of the St Quentin Arch which was exhibited at the Royal Academy in 1925. It is probably a spontaneous sketch recording the design possibly made at a committee meeting or dinner – rather than an initial creative idea. Thumb-nail examples of the latter kind can be seen in plate 65.

67. Preliminary design for the City War Memorial at York, 1924

Pencil on brown paper (630 × 620)

This adventurous design was not accepted; instead a War Cross was set on a formally hedged lawn in Leeman Road. In this design elevations and perspectives show two cenotaphs supporting a stepped, upper portion carrying a bier with a recumbent figure. Lutyens frequently included sculpture in his tombs and monuments and had the ability in his drawings to understand and indicate the general form of a figure that was required.

68. Preliminary design for the Memorial to the Missing of the RAF at Faubourg d'Amiens, Arras, France, for the Imperial War Graves Commission, c1925

Pencil and crayon on detail paper (760 × 1240)

This preliminary study is for the Great Arch in the first rejected design: it represents a tall, stepped bell tower with its four piers set in the form of a Greek cross, resting on an octagonal base. The sheet shows many variations in plan and perspective including thumb-nail sketches for a stepped, interlocking arch similar to the St Quentin-Thiepval scheme (plates 65 and 66).

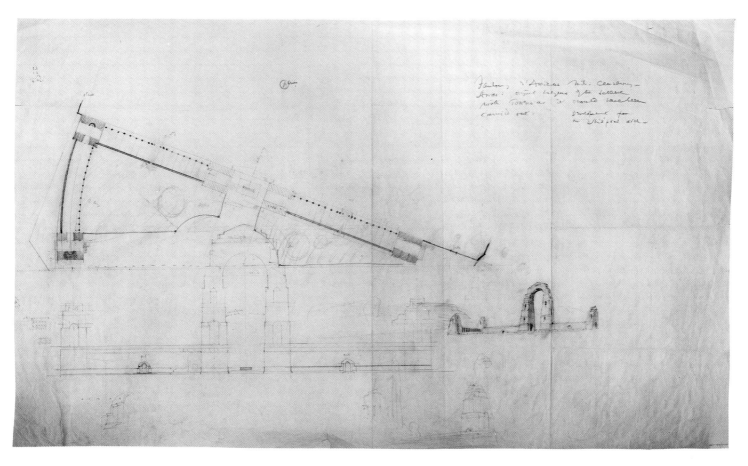

69. Preliminary design for the Cemetery and Memorial to the Missing of the RAF at Faubourg d'Amiens, Arras, France, for the Imperial War Graves Commission, c1925

Pencil and crayon on detail paper (760 × 1270)

The first rejected design took the form of a great stepped arch flanked by adjoining towers, from one of which curves a colonnade to a third tower, the whole group forming the shape of a scythe. The design was far better suited to the awkward site than the memorial which was eventually built, but was rejected on the grounds of expense. Approved in July 1927, the executed design, which Lutyens worked out in December 1925, took the form of a straight cloister, arranged in five bays with six square domed pavilions between them. It was officially opened in 1932.

91

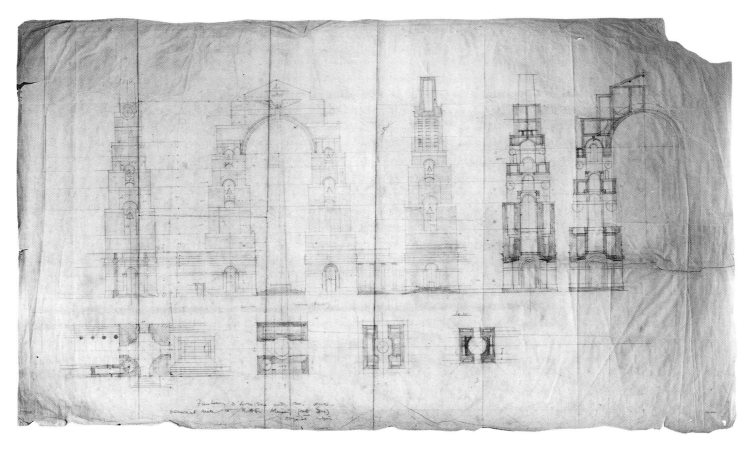

70. Design for the Great Memorial Arch to the Missing of the RAF at Faubourg d'Amiens, Arras, France, for the Imperial War Graves Commission, c1925

Pencil and crayon on detail paper (760 × 1385)

The focal point of the RAF Memorial in the first rejected design was this great stepped arch, very thin and tall. Arched openings containing bells penetrate the side and front elevations alternately at each stage. The arch was a development of Lutyens's design for the St Quentin Memorial to the Missing, his first exercise on this theme, which was rejected in 1927. The drawing is interesting in showing that Lutyens frequently drew up formal designs and working drawings at this stage in his career.

71. Design for the University of London, Bloomsbury, London, 1927

Pencil and crayon on tracing paper (580 × 570)

All through the 1920s there had been plans and discussions about proposed new buildings for London University. Lutyens himself had been involved in 1922, writing on 8 October that 'he had sent some University of London sketches to Hudson'. Then in May 1927 the site was settled when the University purchased ten acres in Bloomsbury. Again Lutyens was involved, noting that he was working on the scheme on 16 July 1927, although he is not mentioned in FLM Thompson's *The University of London 1836-1986*, as being one of the four short-listed

architects. Charles Holden was eventually chosen as the architect in 1931. Lutyens's monumental scheme faced south, bounded on the north by Byng Place, on the east by Woburn and Russell Squares and on the south by Montague Place.

Although he had felt that his Lucknow design was unsuitable for another site, he did in fact partly re-use certain elements in his London scheme – particularly the twin towers and giant arched recesses.

72. **Preliminary study for the Roman Catholic Metropolitan Cathedral of Christ the King, Liverpool, *c* 1929**

Pencil on No 17 Queen Anne's Gate writing paper (200 × 255)

Richard Downey was appointed Archbishop of Liverpool in 1928 and immediately embarked on the project to build a Roman Catholic cathedral for the city, securing a site on Brownlow Hill. In 1929 he approached Lutyens, who undertook the commission and began work on what was to be a cathedral twice as large as St Paul's, London, and in size second only to St Peter's in Rome. At first the project was secret and Lutyens worked on the drawings in private in the racquet court at 13 Mansfield Street. The design was first published in 1930 and then revised before the final scheme was shown to the public in the form of a 17-foot long wooden model which was exhibited at the Royal Academy in 1934.

These early sketches (plates 72-77), made on sheets of writing paper, squared paper and his 'virgins', show the design in evolution. They are some of the one hundred and thirty-four studies gathered together by Harold Greenwood and later acquired by the RIBA in 1980. Greenwood worked alongside Lutyens at Eaton Gate, drawing up the studies to scale, and probably preserved the sketches as Lutyens re-worked and revised the designs.

This worm's-eye perspective of the west front shows a great arched entrance flanked by four openings in a columnar narthex and surmounted by pavilions at either end. The design is close to Lutyens's unexecuted project for Delhi Cathedral (plate 52).

73. **Preliminary study for the Roman Catholic Metropolitan Cathedral of Christ the King, Liverpool, *c*1929**

Pencil and brown crayon on a sheet from his 'virgin' pad (130 × 205)

As the design evolved Lutyens adapted his complex interlocking triumphal arch motif, invented for his first St Quentin project with its high central arch between two lower arches, to the west front and transepts. Two pavilions, later developed as west towers, rise behind the west front.

74. **Preliminary study for the Roman Catholic Metropolitan Cathedral of Christ the King, Liverpool,** *c*1929

Pencil and blue crayon on a sheet from his 'virgin' pad (125 × 205)

This study explores a number of different ideas in a conceptual rather than realistic way: the triumphal arch motif for the west front, the dome and west towers.

**75. Preliminary study for the Roman Catholic
Metropolitan Cathedral of Christ the King,
Liverpool, *c*1929**

Pencil on a sheet from his 'virgin' pad (200 × 125)

Early studies of the dome and its buttresses surmounted by
aedicules.

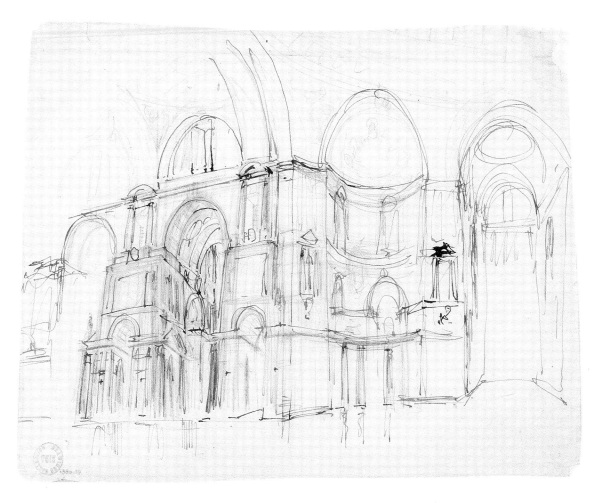

76. Preliminary study for the Roman Catholic Metropolitan Cathedral of Christ the King, Liverpool, *c* 1929

Pencil, pen and coloured crayon on detail paper (305 × 395)

Study of part of the domed central space viewed from the south, showing one of the arched bays of the north nave on the left.

77. **Preliminary study for the Roman Catholic Metropolitan Cathedral of Christ the King, Liverpool, *c*1929**

Pencil, pen and blue crayon on No 13 Mansfield Street writing paper (125 × 203)

The study, which is close to the final design, shows on the left the nave opening into the narthex and, on the right, into the domed central space. In the middle are the three piers of the north side of the nave carrying the two major arches, each pier penetrated by a minor arch. The sketch helps to visualise the three-dimensionality of the complex design which Summerson has described as a series of arches and tunnels driving in each direction through to the outer walls. Work went ahead on the foundations and the crypt, which was finally opened in 1958. Due to a sharp increase in costs Lutyens's designs were then abandoned.

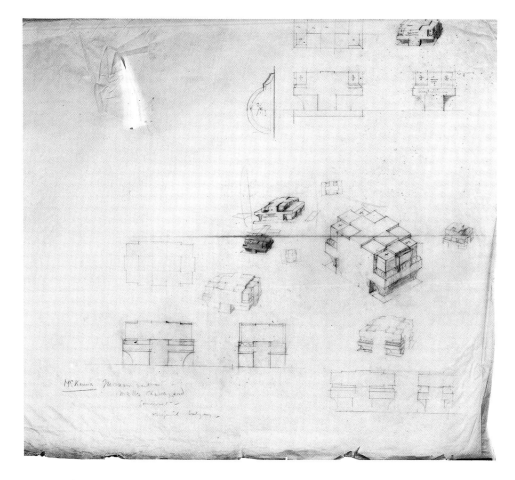

78. Preliminary design for the McKenna family grave in the churchyard of the church of St Andrew, Mells, Somerset, 1932

Pencil on tracing paper (1005 × 1550), detail

The Rt Hon Reginald McKenna, statesman and Chairman of the Midland Bank from 1919 until his death in 1943, first entered Lutyens's circle of friends and clients when he married Pamela Jekyll, daughter of Sir Herbert and niece of Gertrude Jekyll, in 1908. McKenna later introduced Lutyens to the Midland Bank and also privately commissioned No 36 Smith Square (1911), Mells Park House (1924), and Halnaker House (1938). A family grave was commissioned after McKenna's elder son died while a boy at Eton; it eventually took a simpler form, lying between four oaks in the north-east corner of the churchyard.

The design, which is a good example of Lutyens's late 'elemental mode', shows him exploring his idea of interlocking forms in plan, elevations and perspectives from various angles.

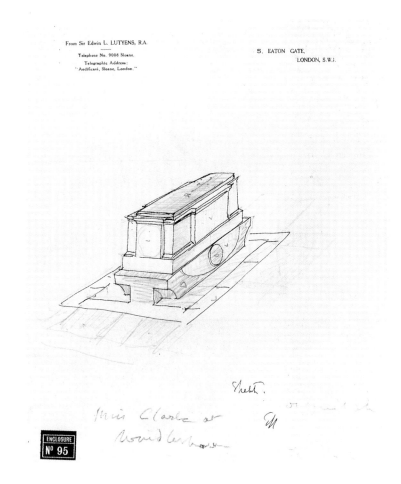

79. **Design for the tomb of Julia Eleanor Clark (1867-1934) in the churchyard of the church of St John the Baptist, Windlesham, Surrey, 1934**

Pencil and pen on No 5 Eaton Gate writing paper (255 × 210)

After the success of the Cenotaph Lutyens was asked to design a great number of small individual memorials and tombstones. The designs for these memorials, both executed and unexecuted, show his range of invention and his re-creation, in abstract form, of traditional tomb types. This sketch, which is virtually as executed, shows his version of the older 'table' tomb. It is built of two colours of travertine marble and is a play of curves and circles, the upper 'tomb' resting on a plinth, which is undercut at either end.

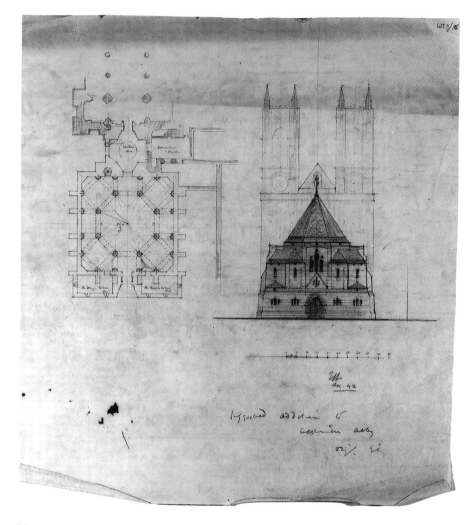

80. **Design for a proposed narthex for Westminster Abbey, London, December 1942**

Pencil and coloured crayon (480 × 455)

This proposal to create a Gothic narthex in front of, and adjoining, the west front of the Abbey was virtually Lutyens's last scheme. Drawn up by the perspectivist, JDM Harvey, it was exhibited at the Royal Academy in May 1943. The reviews were cautious, *The Builder* commenting: 'If he is less successful in his suggested addition to the west end of the Abbey, Wren also found himself less at home there in the Gothic language. It is a question, too, whether the West front of the Abbey should be largely obscured by a new building occupying a valuable open space.'

EDWIN LUTYENS: A CHRONOLOGY

1869   Edwin Landseer Lutyens born in London on 29 March at No 16 Onslow Square, the tenth of the thirteen children of Captain Charles Henry Augustus Lutyens and Mary Gallwey.

1885   Entered the South Kensington School of Art (later the Royal College of Art).

1887   Became an articled pupil to Sir Ernest George and Peto.

1888   Carried out alterations to The Corner, Thursley, Surrey.

1889   Received the commission to design Crooksbury, Farnham, Surrey, for Arthur Chapman; left George's office to set up his own practice; in May met Gertrude Jekyll at Littleworth Cross, who later introduced him to HRH Princess Louise and Edward Hudson of *Country Life*.

1895-96   Designed and built Munstead Wood for Gertrude Jekyll.

1897   Married Lady Emily Lytton on 4 August 1897; designed and built Fulbrook, Elstead, Surrey; Berrydown, Ashe, Hampshire; Orchards, Munstead, Surrey; The Pleasaunce, Overstrand, Norfolk and many other buildings.

1898   Through Sir Herbert Jekyll, Miss Jekyll's brother, he was commissioned to design the British Pavilion for the Paris Exhibition of 1900, which led to a new client in France, Guillaume Mallet, for whom he designed Le Bois des Moutiers at Varengeville.

1899-   After 1900 his schemes became more varied:

1905   Deanery Garden, Sonning, Berkshire (1899); a 'Wren' exercise, the *Country Life* offices, Tavistock Street, London (1904); Neo-Georgian for Nashdom, Taplow, Buckinghamshire (1905). Alterations to two castles: Lindisfarne, Holy Island (1902) and Lambay, Ireland (1905).

1906   Heathcote, Ilkley, Yorkshire, an exercise in Sanmicheli-classicism.

1908   Appointed architect for Hampstead Garden Suburb, where he designed the houses and civic buildings of the central area, St Jude-on-the-Hill and the Free Church.

1909   Appointed consulting architect to the Royal Commission for the International Exhibition at Turin and Rome: Lutyens's Royal Pavilion at Rome (1911) became the British School at Rome.

1910-32   Castle Drogo, Drewsteignton, Devon.

1911-12   Rand Regiments' Memorial and Johannesburg Art Gallery

1912   Elected a member of the Delhi Planning Commission, and set sail for India on the first of nineteen journeys there, on 28 March, to investigate the site and plan of the new city.

1913   In January formally appointed joint architect for New Delhi, with Herbert Baker – Lutyens to design the Viceroy's House and Baker the Secretariats. New Delhi was inaugurated in 1931.

1913   Elected Associate of the Royal Academy.

1917-18   Appointed one of three Principal Architects to the Imperial War Graves Commission, with Herbert Baker and Reginald Blomfield. Designed the Great War Stone (1917); Etaples Military Cemetery (1919); Memorial to the Missing and Cemetery, Faubourg d'Amiens, Arras (1924-25); Memorial to the Missing of the Somme, Thiepval (1926-27) and the Villers-Bretoneux Military Cemetery, Somme (c1927-32), as well as many other cemeteries in France.

1918   Knighted for his work at New Delhi.

1919   Invited by Lloyd George to design a temporary 'catafalque' for the peace procession on 19 July in Whitehall; Lutyens designated it a 'Cenotaph'. It was immediately acclaimed and re-erected in Portland stone on the same site in 1920.

1920   Elected Royal Academician.
Britannic House in the City, for the Anglo-Persian Oil Company, was the first of many post-war commercial commissions in London including buildings for the Midland Bank in Piccadilly (1922), Poultry (1924-39) and Leadenhall Street (1928); Grosvenor House, Park Lane (1926-28); No 68 Pall Mall (1928-29); No 120 Pall Mall (1929-31) and Reuter's, Fleet Street (1935).

1921   Awarded the Royal Gold Medal by the Royal Institute of British Architects. Work began on HM Queen Mary's Dolls' House, which Lutyens designed and co-ordinated.

1924-25   Vice-President of the Royal Institute of British Architects. In 1924 he was awarded the Gold Medal of the American Institute of Architects and became a member of the Royal Fine Art Commission.

1927   British Embassy, Washington.

1929   Commissioned by Richard Downey, Archbishop of Liverpool, to design a new Roman Catholic Cathedral. The Foundation stone was laid on 5 June 1933 and work began on the Crypt, but stopped in 1941. Lutyens's scheme was later abandoned. Sir John Summerson has called his design 'an architectural creation of the highest order, perhaps the latest and supreme attempt to embrace Rome, Byzantium, the Romanesque and the Renaissance in one triumphal and triumphant synthesis'.

1930   Created Knight Commander of the Order of the Indian Empire.

1938   Elected President of the Royal Academy.

1939-42   Worked on the Royal Academy Plan for London.

1941   Awarded the Order of Merit – the first time an architect had received this honour.

1944   Died on 1 January at No 13 Mansfield Street.

PUPILS, ASSISTANTS AND STAFF IN THE LUTYENS OFFICE

(Figures in brackets indicate the length of time served in the office, where known)

1893	William Barlow	1912	Hubert Worthington (Sir) (1912-13)
	Robert Marchant (1893-97)	c1913	William Wands (in office in 1913-c1920; went to Delhi in 1917)
1894	William Henry Ward (1894-98)		
1896	Herbert Luck North (1896-98)	1913	JM Wilson (1913-16), Delhi Raisina Hill office
1897	Maxwell Ormrod Ayrton (1897-1900)	1915	HAN Medd (1915-17)
	John Dalton, secretary (1897-1901)	c1915	Charles Holloway James
	Horace Farquharson (1897-98)	1915	John Greaves, resident representative in Delhi, Raisina Hill office (1915-20)
	Nightingale		
1898	E Baynes Badcock, partner and business manager (1898-1901)	c1915	Clare Nauheim (Lady Railing) (1915 to the mid-1920s, alone with Wands in October 1918)
	John Stevens Lee		
	Kennedy	1917	George Walgate, Delhi Raisina Hill office
	Recketts	c1917	Brandon, Delhi Raisina Hill office
	Davidson	c1917	Purcell Blow
1899	Norman Evill (1899-1902)	c1917	Blomfield, Delhi Raisina Hill office
	John Duke Coleridge (1899-1901)	1919	Herbert Ward (acted as social ADC in South Africa and Delhi, 1919-21)
1900	Samuel Harrington Evans, senior assistant (1900-11, 1913 (Delhi), 1916-c1925)		
			Bertram Carter (1919-22)
1901	Nigel Severne, secretary	1920	Arthur G Shoosmith, resident representative in Delhi Raisina Hill office (1920-31)
	Hon Paul Phipps		
	Richard 'IP' (Infant Prodigy) Huddart		EG Gentry, resident representative in Delhi, Raisina Hill office (1920-28)
	Wallich, American student		
1902	AJ Thomas, business manager (1902-35)	1920	Eadred JT Lutyens, Lutyens's nephew (1920-23)
	Edward E Hall (1902-33)	c1920	Leonard Stedman
	Nicholas 'Beau' Hannen (1902-05)	1921	JJ Ward
	Oswald P Milne (1902-05)	1921	Heathcote G Helmore, from New Zealand (1921-22)
	G Alwyn		
1906	Hughes		Florence Farraghan (Mrs Langford Ellicott), secretary (1921-38)
	Basil G Watney		
1907	George Hartley Goldsmith (1907-10), later worked for the IWGC under Lutyens	c1920s	Harold Greenwood (c1920-44), became Robert Lutyens's partner
		1922	Eleanor Webb, secretary (1922-44)
1910	Humphrey Gimson, nephew of Ernest Gimson (1910-c1913)	1924	WAS Lloyd (1924-27)
			Fred Greenwood (1924-35)
	Verner O Rees (1910-12)	1926	Seton Lloyd (Professor) (1926-27)
c1910-11	Humphrey Chichele Plowden (in office in 1913)		A Trevor Owen (1926-36)
	James Macgregor (in office in 1913)	1927	Robert Heal (1927-30)
	J Anderson (in office in 1913)	c1920s	Hugh Charles Bankart
	ESA Baynes (in office in 1913)		HG Cherry
	HTB Barnard (in office in 1913)	c1928	Hubert Wright, Delhi Raisina Hill office, London office 1938
	Garnet A Farmer (in office in 1913)		
	James Hutton	late 1920s	Alfred Gardner
	James Robertson		
1911	George Stewart (1911-44)	c1932	George Cecil Hough
c1911	JM Easton (c1911)		SG Bailey (c1932-38)
		early 1930s	Basil Spence (Sir)
		1930s	GE Bright

1934	Robert Lutyens (1934-39)	Herbert G Bailey
	Eric Janes (1934-39)	AR Thompson
1935	Hal Kent, from South Africa (1935-37)	AG Gregory (Professor)
	FJ Pook (1935-39)	Macdonald Gill
1930s	Langford Ellicott	Mr and Mrs Percy Tribe, caretakers. Percy Tribe was 'groom-porter' at No 17 Queen Anne's Gate.
	Michael Farey	
late	SW Axford, assistant and Robert Lutyens's	They moved to Eaton Gate and Mansfield Street.
1930s	secretary	Mrs Alice Boyce, housekeeper at No 7 Apple Tree Yard
	R Malya	
	R Walker	
	Christopher Green	

The author is aware that there may be additions to this list and would be glad to receive further information.

SELECT BIBLIOGRAPHY

Books

Lawrence Weaver, *Houses and Gardens by Edwin Lutyens*, Country Life Ltd (London),1913.

Robert Lutyens, *Sir Edwin Lutyens: An Appreciation in Perspective*, Country Life Ltd (London), 1942.

The *Lutyens Memorial* consists of the biography by Christopher Hussey, *The Life of Sir Edwin Lutyens*, and three volumes on the architecture by ASG Butler, *The Architecture of Sir Edwin Lutyens*, Country Life Ltd (London) and Charles Scribner's Sons (New York), 1950.

Margaret Richardson, *Edwin Lutyens*, Catalogue of the Drawings Collection of the Royal Institute of British Architects, Gregg International Ltd (Farnborough), 1973.

Gavin Stamp, *Silent Cities*, RIBA Heinz Gallery exhibition catalogue, London, 1977.

Peter Inskip, *Edwin Lutyens*, Academy Editions (London),1979.

Mary Lutyens, *Edwin Lutyens, by his Daughter*, John Murray (London), 1980.

Daniel O'Neill, *Edwin Lutyens: Country Houses*, Lund Humphries (London) 1980.

Roderick Gradidge, *Edwin Lutyens: Architect Laureate*, George Allen & Unwin (London), 1981.

Robert Grant Irving, *Indian Summer, The Making of New Delhi*, Yale (New Haven and London), 1981.

Colin Amery and Margaret Richardson (eds), *Lutyens*, Arts Council Exhibition Catalogue (London), 1981.

Jane Brown, *Gardens of a Golden Afternoon – The Story of a Partnership, Edwin Lutyens and Gertrude Jekyll*, Allen Lane (London), 1982.

Clayre Percy and Jane Ridley, *The Letters of Edwin Lutyens to his Wife Lady Emily*, Collins (London), 1985.

Christopher Frayling, *The Royal College of Art: One Hundred and Fifty Years of Art and Design*, Barrie and Jenkins (London), 1987.

Jane Brown (ed), *Fulbrook*, Libanus Press (Marlborough), 1989.

Roderick Gradidge, *The Surrey Style*, The Surrey Historic Buildings Trust (Kingston-upon-Thames), 1991.

Articles

Sir Edwin Lutyens, 'What I Think of Modern Architecture', *Country Life*, LXIX, 1931, pp775-77.

Nicholas Pevsner, 'Building with Wit, the Architecture of Sir Edwin Lutyens', *The Architectural Review*, CIX, 1951, pp217-25.

Sir John Summerson, review of the Memorial volumes, *RIBA Journal*, LVIII, 1951, pp390-91.

'Reminiscences on Sir Edwin Lutyens' (a symposium on Lutyens), *Architectural Association Journal*, LXXIV, 1959, pp226-36.

Allan Greenberg, 'Lutyens's Architecture Restudied', *Perspecta*, XII, 1969, pp129-52.

Peter Inskip 'The Compromise of Castle Drogo', *The Architectural Review*, CLXV, 1979 pp220-26.

Gavin Stamp 'The Rise and Fall and Rise of Edwin Lutyens', *The Architectural Review*, CLXX, 1981, pp311-18.

PLATES

1. Design for a boat-house, c1885-87   22
2. Competition design for a village smithy, 1888   23
3. Competition design for a country house, 1888   24
4. Design for alterations to The Corner, Thursley, 1888   25
5. Preliminary design for Crooksbury House, c1889-91   26
6. Design for the gardener's cottage at Littleworth Cross, 1889   27
7. Designs for the gardener's cottage and The Hut at Munstead Wood, c1892-93   28-29
8. Preliminary design for Munstead Wood, c1893   30
9. Preliminary design for north front, Munstead Wood, c1893   31
10. Design for dining-room sideboard, Munstead Wood, c1893   32
11. Preliminary design for south front, Munstead Wood, c1893   33
12. Design for the lodge at Shere Manor House, 1894   34
13. Record sketches of Chinthurst Hill, cmid-1890s   35
14. Design for the entrance to 'Château d'Ease, en Air, sur Fleuve des Rêves', c1895–96   36
15. Preliminary design for additions to the Ferry Inn, 1896   37
16. Design for a garden at East Haddon Hall, 1897   38
17. Design for a proposed house at Mayville, 1897   39
18. Design for a wooden circular seat at Gravetye Manor, 1898   40
19. Design for gardens at Eaton Hall, c1897-98   41
20. Design for the Tea-house sun-dial at Eaton Hall, 1898   42
21. Preliminary design for Methodist Chapel, Overstrand, 1897-98   43
22. Design for Deanery Garden, 1899   44
23. Design for sunken Dutch Garden Court at Orchards, c1899   45
24. Preliminary design for Marshcourt, c1901   46
25. Presentation design for the garden, Abbotswood, 1901   47
26. Preliminary studies for Homewood, Knebworth, 1901   48
27. Preliminary studies for competition designs for St Andrew's Presbyterian Church, Finchley Road, 1901   49
28. Design for a beach estate at Rossall, 1901   50
29. Preliminary studies for Little Thakeham, 1902   51
30. Preliminary design for St John's Institute, 1902   52
31. Design for a house on the Hudson River, 1903   53
32. Preliminary design for the entrance door of the *Country Life* offices, 1904   54
33. Preliminary study for a hotel at Hardelot-Plage, 1905   55
34. Design for Clos du Dan at Varengeville, 1905   56
35. Design for alterations to Ashby St Ledger's, c1904   57
36. Preliminary design for the staircase at Heathcote, 1906   58
37. Preliminary design for the staircase at Heathcote, 1906   59
38. Preliminary design for Viceroy's House, New Delhi, 1912-13   60
39. Preliminary design for Viceroy's House, New Delhi, 1912-13   61
40. Preliminary design for Viceroy's House, New Delhi, 1913-14   62
41. Preliminary design for the Delhi order, Viceroy's House, c1914   63
42. Design for an art gallery bridging the River Liffey, Dublin, 1913   64
43. Preliminary design for the church of St Jude-on-the-Hill, c1909   65
44. Preliminary study for a lodge and gates at Meldon Park, 1909   66
45. Preliminary design for Castle Drogo, 1910   67
46. Preliminary design for Castle Drogo, c1910   68
47. Preliminary design for Castle Drogo, 1911   69
48. Design for Castle Drogo, c1920   70
49. Design for Castle Drogo, c1920   71
50. Design for a mausoleum for the Philipson family, 1914   72
51. Preliminary design for offices for the *Daily Chronicle*, 1914   73
52. Preliminary design for an Anglican Cathedral, New Delhi, 1917   74
53. Preliminary studies for the War Cross, 1918   75
54. Preliminary study for temporary war shrine in Hyde Park, 1918   76
55. Preliminary design for the Cenotaph in Whitehall, 1919   77
56. Preliminary design for the Cenotaph in Whitehall, 1919   78
57. Design for the All-India War Memorial Arch, New Delhi, 1920   79
58. Design for a tower scheme for Britannic House, 1920   80
59. Design for a proposed university at Lucknow, India, c1920-21   81
60. Design for a proposed university at Lucknow, India, c1920-21   82
61. Design for Queen Mary's Dolls' House, 1921   83
62. Rough studies for library furniture in Queen Mary's Dolls' House, c1921   84
63. Design for a royal state-limousine, c1921-24   85
64. Design for the Midland Bank at No 196a Piccadilly, 1922   86
65. Preliminary design for the Memorial at St Quentin, 1923   87
66. Record sketch of design for the Memorial at St Quentin, c1923   88
67. Preliminary design for the City War Memorial at York, 1924   89
68. Preliminary design for the Memorial to the Missing of the RAF at Faubourg d'Amiens, c1925   90
69. Preliminary design for the Cemetery and Memorial to the Missing of the RAF at Faubourg d'Amiens, c1925   91
70. Design for the Great Memorial Arch to the Missing of the RAF at Faubourg d'Amiens, c1925   92
71. Design for the University of London, Bloomsbury, 1927   93
72. Preliminary study for Liverpool Cathedral, c1929   94
73. Preliminary study for Liverpool Cathedral, c1929   95
74. Preliminary study for Liverpool Cathedral, c1929   96
75. Preliminary study for Liverpool Cathedral, c1929   97
76. Preliminary study for Liverpool Cathedral, c1929   98
77. Preliminary study for Liverpool Cathedral, c1929   99
78. Preliminary design for the McKenna family grave, 1932   100
79. Design for the tomb of Julia Eleanor Clark, 1934   101
80. Design for a proposed narthex for Westminster Abbey, 1942   102

(All measurements in the captions are given in millimetres)

INDEX

A

Abbotswood, Stow-on-the-Wold (Gloucs) *47*
Adam, Robert   10
Agra (India)   61
Allingham, Helen   *14*, 30
Alwyn, G   104
Anderson, J   104
Anglo-Persian Oil Company   80
Armstrong, Thomas   11
Ashby St Ledger's (Northants)   *57*
Axford, SW   *4*, 105
Ayrton, Maxwell Ormrod (1874-1960)   14, 104

B

Badcock and Maxey   16
Badcock, E Baynes   15, 16, 104
Bailey, Herbert G   *4*, 105
Bailey, SG   *4*, 104
Baker, Herbert   10, 13, 14, 20, 35, 103
Balfour, Arthur   21
Balfour, Gerald   15, 21
Bankart, Hugh Charles   104
Barlow, William   *14*, 104
Barnard, HTB   104
Barnet, Mrs Henrietta   65
Bath, Pulteney Bridge   64
Battersea, Lord   10, 43
Baynes, ESA   104
Berrydown, Ashe (Hants)   15, 103
Blackburn, Ernest   51
Blagdon Hall (Northumberland)   84
Blomfield, Mr   104
Blomfield, Reginald   103
   Cross of Sacrifice   75
Blomfield, Reginald and Thomas, F Inigo
      The Formal Garden in England (1892)   38
Blow, Purcell   104
Booton (Norfolk)
   The Rectory   43
Boyce, Mrs Alice   105
Brandon, Mr   104
Bray, Sir Reginald   34
Bright, GE   104
Broadbent, Abraham   12, 54
Buckhurst Park (Surrey)   24

Building News Designing Club   23
Busbridge (Surrey)   75
   War Cross   75
Butler, Andrew SG   6, 7, 9, 20, 88
   and Hussey, Christopher *Lutyens Memorial Volumes*   9, 10
      The Architecture of Sir Edwin Lutyens (1950)   9
Butler, Sir Harcourt   81

C

Café Royal   8
Caldecott, Randolph   11, 14
   illustrations for the *Daily Graphic*   11
Cambridge Architectural Society   10
Carter, Bertram (later Secretary of the MARS Group)   18, 21, 104
Castle Drogo, Drewsteignton (Devon)   24, *67, 68, 69, 70, 71*, 103
Castle-in-the-Air sketchbook   14, *36*
Chance, Sir William and Lady   45
Chapman, Mrs Agnes   27
Chapman, Sir Arthur   26, 103
Château d'Ease, Castle-in-the-Air sketchbook   *36*
Cherry, HG   104
Chinthurst Hill, Wonersh (Surrey)   *14*, 24, *35*
Clark, Julia Eleanor, tomb of   *101*
Coleridge, John Duke   104
Cookson, Colonel   66
Corbett, Harvey Wiley   19
Corbusier, Le   10
Country Life   41, 42, 44, 103
Crane, Walter   12
Crooksbury House, Farnham (Surrey)   13, 14, *26*, 103
Curzon, Lord   77, 78

D

Dalton, John   14, 16, 104
Davidson, Mr   104
Dawber, Guy   13
Day, Captain   20
Deanery Garden, Sonning (Berkshire)   *44*, 103
Delhi (India)   16, 17, 18, 19, 35, 60, *80*
   Coronation Durbar, 1911   60
   Delhi order   63
   Planning Commission   60, 103
Delhi, New (India)   *61*, 103
   All-India War Memorial Arch, King's Way   79
   Anglican Cathedral, Queen's Way   74, 94

Secretariats   103
Viceroy's House (now Rashtrapati
   Bhavan)   6, 36, *60, 61, 62, 63*, 79, 103
Dobson   66
Douglas, John   42
Downey, Richard (Archbishop of Liverpool)   94, 103
Drewe, Julius C (founder of the Home and Colonial
   Stores)   67, 68, 69, 70, 71
   ancestor, Drogo de Teynton   67
Drewsteignton (Devon), Castle Drogo   24, *67, 68, 69, 70, 71*, 103
Dublin
   Gallery bridging the River Liffey   36
   Irish War Memorial   19
   Municipal Art Gallery   64

E

East Haddon Hall (Northants)
   gardens and garden features   *38*
Easton, John Murray   104
Eaton Hall (Cheshire)
   gardens   *41*
   Tea-house sun-dial   *42*
Ellicott, Langford   105
Elstead (Surrey), Fulbrook   15, 16, 103
Elwin, the Reverend Whitwell   43
Etaples Military Cemetery (France)   78, 103
Eton   100
Evans, Edmund   11
Evans, Samuel Harrington (*c*1877-1961)   104
Evill, Norman   104

F

Falkner, Harold   12, 20
Farey, Cyril   19
Farey, Michael (son of Cyril Farey)   105
Farmer and Brindley   42
Farmer, Garnet A   104
Farnham (Surrey), Crooksbury House   13, 14, *26*, 103
Farquharson, Horace (1875-1966)   104
Farraghan, Florence (Mrs Langford Ellicott)   104
Farrer, Gaspard and Henry   17
Fatehpur-Sikri (India)   61
Faubourg d'Amiens, Arras (France)
   Memorial to the Missing of the RAF   *90, 91, 92*, 103
Fenwick, Mark   47
Foster, Birket   14, 30
Fountain, Mr (amateur architect)   43
Frensham (Surrey)   11

Fulbrook, Elstead (Surrey)   15, 16, 103
Fulbrook sketchbook   14

G

Gallwey, Mary (Mrs CHA Lutyens)   10, 103
Gardner, Alfred   104
Gentry, EG   104
George, Lloyd   77, 103
George, Sir Ernest   7, 13, 14, 26, 27, 35
   Harpenden (Herts)
      Redcote   25
George, Sir Ernest and Peto   13, 25, 103
   Batsford Park (Gloucs)   13
   Collingham Gardens (London)   13
   Harrington Gardens (London)   13
   office at No 18 Maddox Street (London)   13
George V, King   60
Gibbons, Grinling   54
Gill, Macdonald   105
Godalming (Surrey)
   Milford House   36
   Tickner's builders' yard   11
Goddards, Abinger (Surrey)   15, 30
Godwin, EW   11, 20
   sketchbook   20
Goldsmith, George Hartley (1886/7-1967)   104
Gould, Mr (George's office manager)   13
Gravetye Manor
   design for a circular seat   *40*
Gray, Edmund   25
Great Maytham (Kent)   12
Greaves, John M   104
Green, Christopher (son of W Curtis Green)   105
Greenaway, Kate   11
Greenwood, Fred   104
Greenwood, Harold (1904-1972)   *4, 9*, 94, 104
Greenwood, Mrs Alison   9, 12
Gregory, (Professor) AG   105
Guest, Hon Ivor (later second Viscount Wimborne)   57
Guthrie, David Charles   38
Guthrie, Miss Aemilia   35

H

Hall, Edward E   16, 17, 18, 104
Halnaker House (Sussex)   100
Hampton Court (Middx)   54
Hampton Court Bridge (Middx)   20
Hannen columbarium, Wargrave (Bucks)   72

Hannen, Nicholas 'Beau'   104
Hardelot-Plage, Pas de Calais (France)
   hotel   *55*
Harriman, Averell   53
Harriman, Mr EH (railway millionaire)   *4*, 53
Harriman, Mrs EH   53
Harvey, JDM   102
Hascombe (Surrey), Sullingstead   15
Heal, Robert   19, 104
Heathcote, Ilkley (Yorkshire)   *58, 59*, 103
Helmore, Heathcote G (1894-1965)   104
Hemingway, Ernest   58, 59
Hirsel, The (Berwickshire)   12
Holden, Charles   93
Home, Earl of   12
Homewood, Knebworth (Herts)   *48*
Hore-Belisha   19
Hough, George Cecil (*fl* 1929-60)   104
Huddart, Richard (IP Infant Prodigy)   104
Hudson, Edward   44, 54, 93, 103
Hudson River, New York (house on)   *4, 53*
Hughes, Mr   104
Humphrey Gimson (nephew of Ernest Gimson)   104
Hussey, Christopher   9, 10, 12, 16, 17, 20, 29
   and Butler, Andrew *Lutyens Memorial Volumes*   9, 10
   The Life of Sir Edwin Lutyens (1950)   7, 9, 12, 20, 21
Hutton, James   104

I

Ikley (Yorkshire), Heathcote   *58, 59*, 103
Imperial War Graves Commission   18, 75, 79, 87, 90, 91, 92, 103
India, Viceroy of   60, 61. *See also* Delhi, New (India): Viceroy's House (now
   Rashtrapati Bhavan)
Inskip, Peter   69

J

James, Charles Holloway (1893-1953)   104
Janes, Eric   *4*, 105
Jekyll, Gertrude   15, 27, 28, 29, 31, 32, 41, 47, 83, 100, 103
   Home and Garden (1900)   31
   Old West Surrey (1904)   29
Jekyll, Pamela   100
Jekyll, Sir Herbert   103
Johannesburg (South Africa)
   Johannesburg Art Gallery   64, 103
   Rand Regiment's Memorial   103
Johnson, Herbert   46

K

Kennedy, Mr   104
Kent, Hal   15, 19, 105
Knebworth (Herts), Homewood   *48*

L

Lambay Castle (Ireland)   103
Landseer, Sir Edwin   10, 11
Lane, Sir Hugh   64
Langley, Batty
   City and Country Builder's and Workman's Treasury   17, 51
Lantéri, Edward   12
Le Touquet-Paris-Plage (France), Mayville   *39*, 55
Lee, John Stevens   104
Lee, Sir Austin   53
Lindisfarne Castle (Northumberland)   103
Little Thakeham (Sussex)   17, *51*
Littleworth Cross, Seale (Surrey)   *27*, 103. *See also* Squirrel Hill
Liverpool
   Roman Catholic Metropolitan Cathedral   *4*, 9, 19, 20, 36,
      63, *94, 95, 96, 97, 98, 99*, 103
Lloyd, (Professor) Seton   104
Lloyd, WAS   104
London
   Bloomsbury, University of London   *93*
   Britannic House, Finsbury Circus   18, *80*, 103
   Byng Place   93
   Country Life offices, Nos 2-10 Tavistock Street   12, 54, 103
   Eaton Gate (No 5)   9, 18, 19, 28, 94, 101
   Fleet Street, Reuter's   73, 103
   Finchley, St Andrew's Presbyterian Church   *49*
   Finsbury Circus, Brittanic House   18, *80*, 103
   Golders Green Crematorium, Philipson family mausoleum   *72*
   Greenwich Hospital   81
   Grosvenor House, Park Lane   103
   Hampstead Garden Suburb, Barnet   50, 65, 103
      Central Square   65
      Free Church   103
      Institute   65
      St Jude-on-the-Hill   *65*, 103
   Hyde Park, temporary war shrine   *76*
   Imperial War Museum   21, 77
   Kensington Palace   37
   London County Hall   36
   Mansfield Street (No 13)   9, 18, 20, 94, 99, 103
   Midland Bank
      Leadenhall Street   103
      Piccadilly (No 196a)   *86*, 103

Spencer, Colonel 14, 16
Squirrel Hill, Seale (Surrey) 27
St Quentin, Nord (France)
    Memorial to the Missing *87, 88, 90*, 92, 95
        model at the Royal Academy 88
Stedman, Leonard 104
Stevenson, JJ 28
Stewart, George *4*, 9, 16, 104
Stockbridge (Hants), Marshcourt 12, *46*
Stone of Remembrance, Great War 75
Stow-on-the-Wold (Gloucs), Abbotswood *47*
Sullingstead, Hascombe (Surrey) 15
Summerson, Sir John 99, 103

T

Taplow (Bucks), Nashdom 103
Temple Dinsley (Herts) 12
Thiepval, Somme (France)
    Memorial to the Missing 87, 88, 90, 103
Thomas, AJ 15, 16, 17, 18, 21, 104
Thompson, AR *4*, 105
Thompson, FLM
    The University of London 1836-1986 93
Thursley (Surrey) 11
    The Corner 25, 103
    The Cottage 11
Tonks, Henry (Head of the Slade School) 12
Tribe, Mr and Mrs Percy *4*, 18, 105

U

United Newspapers Ltd 73

V

Varengeville, near Dieppe (France)
    Clos du Dan *56*
    Le Bois des Moutiers 39, 56, 103
    Les Communes 56
Versailles 54
Venice
    Rialto Bridge 64
Victoria Memorial competition *49*
Victoria, Queen 21, 37, 83
Villers-Bretoneux cemetery, Somme (France) 19, 103

W

Walcot, William 19
Wales, Prince of 11

Walgate, George 104
Walker, JC (clerk of works at Castle Drogo) 71
Walker, R *4*, 105
Wallich, Mr 104
Wands, William 104
War Cross 75
    Busbridge (Surrey) 75
    Wargrave (Berks) 75
Ward, JJ 104
Ward, Rev Herbert 104
Ward, William Henry (1865-1924) 14, 104
Wargrave (Berks)
    Hannen columbarium 72
    War Cross 75
Waring, SJ (of Waring & Gillow) 76
Washington (USA)
    British Embassy 63, 103
Waterhouse, Alfred 41
Watney, Basil G (?-1915) 104
Weaver, Lawrence 44
    Memorials and Monuments (1915) 75
Webb, Barbara (Mrs Robert) 36
Webb, Eleanor *4*, 18, 20, 104
Westminster, Duke of 11, 15, 41, 42
Whinney, Son and Austen Hall 86
Whistler, Laurence 21
Whitley, John Robinson 39, 55
Wilberforce, Archdeacon 52
Wilson, JM 104
Windlesham (Surrey)
    Clark tomb at Church of St John the Baptist *101*
Windsor Castle 15, 83
Wood, RA (of JW Falkner Ltd) 9, 14, 28
Wonersh (Surrey), Chinthurst Hill 14, 24, *35*
Worthington, (Sir) Hubert 104
Wren, Sir Christopher 52, 54, 81, 86, 102, 103
Wright, Hubert *4*, 104

Y

Yates, Cook and Darbyshire 19
Yeats, WB 64
York
    City War Memorial, Leeman Road *89*

Z

Zumbach, Albert (Miss Jekyll's Swiss gardener) 29